NATIVE AMERICAN LIFE

NATIVE AMERICAN LIFE

THE FAMILY, THE HUNT, PASTIMES AND CEREMONIES

COLIN F. TAYLOR Ph.D

SMITHMARK

This edition published in 1996 by
SMITHMARK Publishers,
a division of U.S. Media Holdings, Inc.,
16 East 32nd Street,
New York, NY 10016.

9 8 7 6 5 4 3 2 1

SMITHMARK books are available for bulk purchase for sales promotion and premium use. For details write or call the manager of special sales, SMITHMARK Publishers, 16 East 32nd Street, New York, NY 10016; (212) 532-6600.

Produced by Salamander Books Ltd
129-137 York Way
London N7 9LG
United Kingdom

ISBN 0-8317-7334-0

Printed in the United Kingdom
by Butler & Tanner Ltd, Frome and London

CREDITS
Project Editor: Christopher Westhorp
Designer: Mark Holt
Editor: Joyce Willcocks
Map: Janos Marffy (© Salamander Books Ltd)
Filmset: SX Composing Ltd, England
Color reproduction: Pixel Tech Ltd, Singapore

AUTHOR

Colin F. Taylor Ph.D is a Senior Lecturer at Hastings College of Art and Technology, Hastings, England. He is acknowledged as a leading expert on Plains Indian culture and his previous books include *Native American Myths and Legends, Native American Arts and Crafts* and Smithmark's highly successful *The Native Americans*.

Page 1: A Zuni jar from 1890, black and red on white with a sloping neck and smaller rim with representations of two fire clouds.
Page 2: A collection of everyday objects: clockwise, from bottom left: Quinault rush mat, Eskimo snow goggles, Paiute ceremonial basket, Tlingit horn spoon, Esquimaux walrus ivory-handled chopping blade, Chinook wooden comb with mask handle, Zuni jar, Cherokee girl's doll, Iroquois racket, Passamaquoddy ball, and Comanche boy's moccasins.
Page 5: A Kwakiutl house post carved to represent the 'speaker' of the house.

CONTENTS

INTRODUCTION

THE FIRST TWO volumes in this series have documented the rich mythology and arts and crafts of the North American Indians[1]. Continuing the theme, this book now looks at the traditional family life of the native people as it existed, in its many diversified forms, among the hundreds of tribes within the nine recognized cultural regions of North America.[2] The lifestyles described are largely as they were prior to the impact of, and changes brought about by, European colonization. This change commenced in October 1492 when Columbus' expedition reached San Salvador (an island in the present-day Bahamas) and some 20 years later, in 1513, when the Spanish set up a colony on the American continent in the region which is now known as Florida.

By the late 1500s, both the French and English had founded colonies on the mainland, and, fascinated by what they had learned, two artists, Jacques le Moyne de Morgues and John White,

were commissioned to map, document and make pictorial records of the Indians and their various lifestyles. John White was one of Sir Walter Raleigh's colonists who made several trips to 'Virginia'[3] between 1585 and 1590; a superb artist, he – as with Le Moyne in the Florida region a few years earlier – made a number of highly accurate paintings of the Algonquian tribes who lived in the region of Roanoake Island and the nearby mainland of what later became North Carolina.

The paintings, which still survive today in the British Museum, were produced with meticulous attention to detail, recording for posterity the incredible richness of New World daily life. Thus, the Indian village of *Pomeiooc* – not far from present-day Jamestown – had rectangular houses covered with mats and bark, some of which could be turned back to admit light (see page 15 for an engraving based on White's painting). A larger dwelling identified the chief's house which was

A Navajo woman (right) combs her husband's long hair with a brush of bunch grass, a tool which would also be employed to tamp the weft elements into position on the partially finished blanket visible on the loom to the right. Although posed, the scene shows much of Navajo culture – hairstyle, costume, silver conchas and weaving, as well as the desert environment and sculptured mesas of their Southwest homeland.

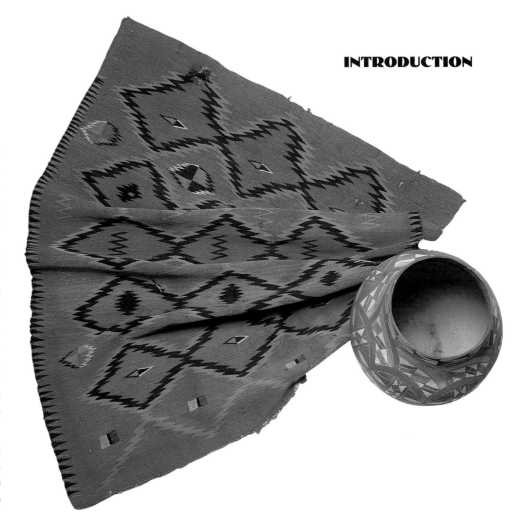

adjacent to a central village plaza – an area used as a meeting place for feasts and ceremonials. Also prominent was, as White described it, 'a temple', differing from the other buildings in that it was round, domed and covered with hides instead of mats and bark.

That horticulture was important to these Algonquians is testified by White's illustrations and descriptions of gardens in 'neat array'[4] at *Pomeiooc*, as well as at the other village, *Secoton*, which White visited. Fortifications, irrigation, complex ceremonial, child life, women's clothing, men's weapons, dance, feasts, mortuary customs, shamans and priests, modes of hunting and fishing, utensils, methods of cooking, and even the use of chastity belts, were carefully recorded by this perceptive and dedicated observer.

These illustrations reached a wide audience in Europe through the careful engravings produced by the opportunist Flemish publisher Theodor De Bry in 1590; without question, they caught the

The Southwest was a region rich in arts and crafts, especially pottery and weaving. As with many traditional crafts people, there existed a marked ability to beautify a commonly used household object and imbue it with a spirit and life of its own – as with this Navajo blanket and pueblo jar (above).

These Hopi girls (left) are making cornbread in traditional fashion. As well as a foodstuff, corn was made into a sacred form of cornbread called *piki* which was used in ceremonies. Also, the morning was often greeted by a sprinkling of corn pollen directed at the rising sun.

Some regions were mild throughout the year, others were very hot in summer and exceedingly cold in winter. This scene from a winter camp (above) was photographed at the turn of the century. A well-lined and -heated *tipi* was warm and comfortable, although heavy buffalo rugs were also needed during the coldest periods.

imagination of the Old World much as a similar pictorial record of life on some distant planet would impact on the world today.

With time contacts widened, giving further glimpses of Indian life. The immense interest generated was partially satisfied by the visit in 1616 of such notables as *Pocahontas*, daughter of the powerful chief *Powhatan*,[5] who also sent his adviser, *Uttamatomakkin*, to 'investigate the homeland of the English'[6] – clearly, there was interest on both sides!

The year 1710 saw the visits of the four Mohawk 'Kings' to London, elaborately tattooed and garbed in native dress – moccasins decorated with quillwork, belts of bark and nettle cord decorated with moosehair, ancient weapons and

elaborate hairstyles – they told much of the lifestyle of the indigenous Americans.

The pattern was to be repeated countless times over the next three centuries as fur traders, travelers, scientists and artists progressively moved west from the Atlantic shores[7]. One of the most prolific of these individuals was the artist and writer, George Catlin, who – traveling to nearly 50 different tribes in the period 1832-1839 – produced over 300 paintings in oil documenting 'their games and religious ceremonies – their dances – their ball plays – their buffalo hunting,....their costumes, and all their other manufactures, from the size of a wigwam down to the size of a quill or a rattle'[8]. The following pages illustrate several of Catlin's depictions of North

American Indian daily life, and while generally less detailed than John White's observations of the Algonquians on the Atlantic seaboard some two and a half centuries previously, they parallel his observations and are invaluable records of rich cultures all but gone.

As the record unfolded, although there were considerable variations in bodily proportions and stature, all American Indians were observed to exhibit straight black hair, a skin of various shades of brown, a tendency to the Mongoloid eyefold and high prominent cheekbones, which led one Spanish observer to comment 'If we have seen one American, (Indian) we may be said to have seen all, their color and make are so nearly alike'[9]. Universally, eyes were light to dark brown while facial and body hair was, on the whole, less pronounced than with the average white person, moustache and beard being generally sparse. Physically, the hips, thighs and calves were smaller than the average white's, as were the feet and hands.[10]

The Eskimo differed considerably in several anatomical features, the skin generally being yellow or very light brown, and while hair and eyes, as with Indians, were dark, the eyes were obliquely set, the nasal bones were particularly narrow and the face large and flat. Since there was considerable intermarriage, several of these characteristics were also exhibited by adjacent Indian tribes in the Subarctic region.

Obviously, to a considerable extent, studies of the past must rest firmly on the scholarship of many individuals – both amateur and professional – who observed and recorded the lifestyles of the peoples they encountered, as exemplified by the superb 16th century studies of Jacques le Moyne de Morgues and John White which were discussed earlier.

However, these valuable records have been extended here by reference to Native American 'texts', such as pictographs, dry-paintings, totem poles and other carvings, oral history, wampum belts, winter counts and, where possible, the direct information from the people themselves, as

The storage bags created by the Nez Perce (left, center) were some of the most distinctive and identifiable designs on the continent. Made of hemp and corn husk, this bag dates from 1885. Just as these cornhusk bags were a Plateau speciality, so pipe bags were a Plains speciality. This Cheyenne example (left) belonged to Short Bear and is made of leather, beads, and quills; it dates from 1910.

The Northwest Coast culture was a highly developed one, not least their totemic culture and stress on wealth and status. This view of the Haida village of Skidegate (below) shows the dramatic impact of poles. Even everyday items were decorated; this Tlingit halibut hook (above), for example.

recorded by competent researchers such as Alice Fletcher and Francis La Flesche for the Omaha and Frances Densmore for the Chippewa.[11]

In addition, the artifacts illustrated here, have been viewed as cultural and historical 'documents', which when studied can give important insights into, and evoke sentiments relating to, the lives of the people who produced them. Thus, the Hidatsa hoe (page 67), tells of a horticultural lifestyle; the Cherokee rackets (page 49) evoke the importance of ball play to this Southeastern tribe – as vividly described by George Catlin in 1834 (see Recreation and Pastimes); the *Yei* rug (page 36) the Navajo's complex dry-painting designs which encapsulated much of their cosmos, while the Eskimo lamp (page 58) underlines the importance of a *single* flame to maintain life within an Arctic habitation.

Several volumes would be needed to document fully the wide variety of lifestyles in the nine cultural areas considered; the attempt here has been to examine some of the most interesting and key facets of the cultures, touching on social organization, the transmission of knowledge – history, religion and ceremonial – recreation and pastimes, the home and domestic life, trade patterns, methods of hunting and styles of warfare, and, finally, the changes wrought as the Euroamerican expansion took effect.

Some echoes of this past lifeway can still be gleaned when one travels to the reserves and reservations in Canada and the United States today, where elements of traditional habitations, foods, song, dance, ceremonial, costume, games and language, may be experienced. But the past is largely a 'foreign land' – they did things so much differently then![12]

The daily lives discussed in this volume embrace the nine major cultural areas of North America (above). The boundaries are, of course, fluid rather than rigid and the map thus serves to delineate them approximately. They are: Southeast (**1**), Southwest (**2**), Plains (**3**), Plateau and Basin (**4**), California (**5**), Northwest Coast (**6**), Subarctic (**7**), Arctic (**8**), and Northeast (**9**).

TRIBAL AND SOCIAL ORGANIZATION

'If you reverence the aged, many will be glad to hear of your name...The poor man will say to his children,"my children, let us go to him, for he is a great hunter, and is kind to the poor, he will not turn us away empty," The Great Spirit, who has given the aged a long life, will bless you.'

COPWAY (OJIBWA)[1]

THERE WERE WIDELY differing forms of government among the North American Indians, varying from the simplest family group and village community to complex confederations of highly organized tribes.

Thus, in the case of the tribes of California, the social and political structure was simple and above the direct family the only definite units of organization were the villages, with common bonds of language and frequency of interaction. Fairly typical for tribes of northern California, is the political and social organization of the Karok who occupied the middle course of the Klamath River and who shared a similar organization to that of the adjacent Yurok and Hupa. Here, within the village, it was the rich men who were the leaders but there were no chiefs in the ordinary sense, the community being regulated by the set of values shared by its members, and family life was organized within a framework of the kinship system. Of interest is the fact that the Karok world view recognized no crimes against the tribe or the community. Individualism was strongly encouraged and a person could steal, even murder, without actually being stigmatized as a criminal. The explanation for what was undesirable behavior, was interpreted as a transgression against the supernatural which would bring bad luck, while transgression against private persons would have to be paid for in the form of some indemnity to the offended individuals. If the violator refused to pay, he was likely to be killed by those he had offended and this killing could in turn result either in indemnification, or in further violence between the families concerned.[2] As one observer put it, 'If the money is paid without higgling, the slayer and the avenger at once became boon companions. If not, the avenger must have the murderer's blood, and a system of retaliation is initiated which would be without end were it not that it may be arrested at any moment by the payment of money'.[3]

The political organization of the Maidu to the south and east of the Karok was, however, somewhat more complex with an elected village headman who was assisted by the leader of each of the extended families. They took various roles and also acted as 'official host at ceremonial gatherings and supervised accumulation, preparation, and distribution of food'.[4]

A decided feature of northern Californian social and political organization was a great emphasis on wealth and social position. The Hupa, for example, accumulated wealth not only by shell currency but also by albino or unusually colored deerskins, large blades of imported red or black obsidian, and elaborate headdresses of woodpecker feathers.[5] These rare and precious objects being displayed at group festivals.

The organization of the Eskimo paralleled much of that of the Californian tribes and in matters of government, each village settlement tended to be independent. Within the villages, most families also tended to be independent

In most cultures children were instructed from an early age as to what was expected of them in adulthood; boys were taught by their fathers and girls by their mothers. This Crow girl (main picture) is holding a miniature cradle complete with a doll, just as a mother would hold a real child. Note that the doll has a porcelain head and is of European origin. A richly decorated, full-sized example of a Plains cradle (above left) – identified as Lakota but perhaps Cheyenne – illustrates the use of a relatively simple construction techique combined with lavish embellishment to create an object of great beauty. The manufacture of clothing was almost wholly a female task, the intricate 'big shirt' designs, like that seen here (right and far left), being a speciality of the Seminole.

This somewhat idealized painting (right) shows the Spanish explorer Hernando De Soto reaching the banks of the Mississippi River in 1540 during his explorations of the southwest and encountering the Indian tribes living in the vicinity – their first sight of a horse. The contact was brutal – De Soto kidnaped local chiefs and held them hostage for food and slaves – and heralded disaster for many of the native peoples in the region, and beyond, through which he traveled.

although there was considerable coordination between groups in fishing and hunting and there was generally a recognized headman, *umialik*, who, supported by the family leaders, made decisions in certain matters, such as the change of village site. The *umialik* and the council, consisting of family representatives, arbitrated in both intratribal and intertribal affairs. In addition there was involvement in the resolving of theft and murder – punishment consisting of ostracism, banishment or even execution by the wronged family; this death sanction 'often resulted in a long-standing feud between families'.[6]

Tribal Confederacies

In sharp contrast to California and the Subarctic were the powerful confederacies formed by several groups mainly in the eastern part of North America, the earliest recorded being that of

the so-called Powhatan confederacy of the Virginian Algonquian tribes whose territory included the tidewater section of Virginia from the Potomac and south to the James River near present-day Richmond. The confederacy was first mentioned by the Spaniards as early as 1570 and occupied at that time more than 200 villages. The confederacy was founded by a certain *Wahunsonacock* probably sometime toward the end of the 15th century. This man is best known to history as Powhatan and the confederacy was named after him.[7] An important element in the political structure of the confederacy was the paying of tribute to Powhatan who made personal visits throughout his territory to collect it. The 'tribute' which consisted of the products of the field and chase as well as beads and copper not only centered the wealth of the confederacy with Powhatan but also served as a continuous acknowledgment of the submission of the lesser chiefs to Powhatan 'and of their readiness to fol-low him to his wars'.[8] He was viewed as a 'king and as a half god' instilling great fear among the populace. 'Severe beatings were given for ordi-nary corrections, and horrible death by fire, by piecemeal amputation, or by clubbing constituted the punishment for more serious offenses'.[9]

Somewhat looser in their political structures and certainly far less dictatorial were such alliances as the Seven Council Fires of the Dakota and the Three Fires – Potawatomi, Ottawa and Chippewa – of the western Great Lakes region. In the southeast was the powerful Caddoan confed-eracy which, when first encountered by the Spanish explorer De Soto in 1540, occupied the region of present-day Louisiana and Arkansas.[10]

League of the Iroquois

Without doubt the best-organized and most democratic alliances were the Iroquoian confed-eracies of the Northeast, such as the famed League of the Iroquois and the lesser-known Huron confederation of four tribes which appears to have been founded at least as early as the first

quarter of the 17th century, in a desperate bid to counter the relentless war waged on them by the Iroquois to their east, who by the 1650s all but destroyed them as a tribe.

According to Iroquois tradition, there was once a time when all the tribes of the region were in conflict with one another and in order to end this virtually continuous state of war, the Great Peace or Confederacy of the Iroquois was established. The confederation referred to themselves as 'People of the Longhouse' and 'In this Longhouse, the Senecas, the most western of the Iroquois, were designated the Keepers of the Western Door and the Mohawks, the most eastern, the Keepers of the Eastern Door',[11] while the other three tribes (Oneida, Onondaga, and Cayuga) were arranged in a line between them.[12]

The 'aged sensible' Woman

A council composed of some 50 chiefs or sachems, all of equal rank and selected from the maternal families, administered the affairs of the League. These chiefs assembled whenever necessity arose, such as to decide on peace or war with other tribes, to discuss intertribal problems or to receive outside ambassadors or delegations. The chiefs were strictly federal officials and had no legal authority in any matters that concerned a single clan or tribe. Of particular interest is the fact that it was the senior *woman* of the clan, an 'aged sensible' woman,[13] who, in consultation with other women belonging to that clan, initially selected a prospective sachem who, after approval by other sachems was installed in office at a special intertribal festival. As one authority has observed, the same 'aged sensible' woman 'had power to depose him again if he failed to uphold the dignity of his position'.[14]

The great councils of the confederacy were gen-erally called by the Onondaga, the most centrally placed of the five tribes, and each year the 'Nations of the Confederacy were drawn from their respective council fires to the *great* council fire at Onondaga, to rehearse their ancient sys-tems and compose their differences'.[15]

Limited war was waged relentlessly and almost continuously between the Iroquois and Huron confederacies in the heavily wooded parts of eastern North America. As a protective measure people generally lived in well-stocked, palisaded villages similar to that of the Algonquian village of Pomelooc depicted here (left). The entrances were narrow and well-guarded, and the palisades might be 20ft (6m) high and double or triple. Note the bark- and mat-covered longhouses, the typical domestic buildings of the region. The chief's dwelling is the large house at the left.

Women were important in transmitting cultural values but their lives were far from easy and invariably they worked far harder than their menfolk did. This was sometimes compensated for by the status of women in particular societies where they controled blood descent, titles of chieftainship, clan lands, and so on. These Arapaho women and girls (below) were pictured at the turn of the century in Oklahoma at an exposition. Note the range of dresses worn – buckskin, beaded and painted skin and cowrie shell decor types.

It was the Onondaga too who became the keepers of the tribal archive that was held traditionally in the form of wampum belts which acted as memory aids for important events of the League, such as treaties between other tribes and Europeans.[16]

Confederacies on the Plains

As well as the seven council fires of the Dakota, another loosely knit confederacy on the Plains was that of the Blackfeet, who ranged over an immense area: east of the Rockies from the Saskatchewan River in present-day Alberta to the headwaters of the Missouri River. Consisting of the Blackfeet proper or *Siksika*, the Piegan or *Pikuni*, and the Blood or *Kainah*, they were recognized by early explorers as separate tribes, each generally politically independent. However, as one scholar observed, they shared the same customs (with the exception of a few ceremonial rituals), intermarried, and made war upon common enemies: 'So it has been customary to speak of these three tribes as one people,[17] . . . [and]

together these three tribes comprised the strongest military power on the north-western plains in historic buffalo days'.[18]

In common with other nomadic Plains groups, the three tribes of the confederacy were split up into bands each of which had a headman who was chosen not only for his leadership abilities but who was also in possession of considerable wealth which he was willing to dispense for the public good. In turn, each of the tribes had a head chief who was elected by the general agreement of the headmen and all important matters were generally decided in the councils of the various band leaders and heads of the powerful military societies, under the direction of the head chiefs.

A similar alliance was formed on the southern Plains in the 1840s – intertribal warfare in the region being largely eliminated – so that the warriors' best energies could be directed against the white and other intruders.[19]

Women's Status

Romance was by no means lacking in the sex life of the North American Indian but, as with many societies, there were often double standards. Thus, while young men were almost everywhere rather expected to be philanderers, the behavior of young women was carefully watched and almost without exception chastity was very highly regarded. Virtuous esteemed women, particularly among the Plains tribes, were sought for tasks of honor at the sacred ceremonials, such as the Holy Woman in the Blackfeet Sun Dance[20] and the four Lakota women who ceremonially cut the tree for the Sun Dance pole.[21]

Among the Iroquoian tribes – which include the Huron and Susquehanna – the penalties for killing a woman of the tribe were double those exacted for the killing of a man, it being recognized that there was an acute loss of a long line of prospective offspring. In contrast, however – and this illustrates the difficulties of attempting to generalize – with the Northwest Coast Indians, the penalty for killing a woman of the tribe, was half that of killing a man.[22]

Early observers have reported on the brutality sometimes meted out to women in several cultural areas, thus Hardesty reports that in the case of the Loucheux of the Subarctic 'the women are literally beasts of burden to their lords and masters. All the heavy work is performed by them'.[23] These sentiments are similar to those reported by Samuel Hearne in 1770 who was befriended by the Chipewyan chief, Mattonabee. Great misfortune had overtaken Hearne's fur trading expedition to the region of the Great Slave Lake; this, Mattonabee claimed, was due to the lack of women in the party and he lectured Hearne on their value since they were 'made for labor', that one of them could haul or carry as much as two men and that they could not only erect the tents and see to the fires at night but could be kept at minimum expense since – and this was obviously added with an element of sadistic humor – they were also the cooks, the 'very licking of their fingers' in scarce times would be quite sufficient for the subsistence![24]

In more recent years, government policies of the 1950s threatened termination of the reservations and relocation of the people. It put enormous pressures on Indian women to deny their Indian identity and lose their traditional way of life. But Indian women confronted the challenge and from the 1970s great emphasis was put on 'the reclamation of their cultural and political autonomy'. Thus, a number of Indian women's organizations were formed in the 1970s and 1980s in an attempt to circumvent 'the extraordinary assaults on native culture'.[25] As Karen Olsen, an Inuit scholar observed, women were traditionally instrumental in maintaining cultural values – respect for the land and animals and ritual ceremonial – and this theme has been increasingly revitalized both by female Indian youths and elders. Typical is Agnes Vanderburg, a Salish teacher and elder, who has founded cultural camps to teach the ancient skills of her people – such as the tanning of hides and the use of traditional foods.[26] The movement is summed up by a contemporary woman's poem 'Remember':

'Remember the sky that you were born under,
know each of the star's stories . . .
Remember the plants, trees, animal life who
all have their tribes, their families, their
histories, too...

JOY HARJO (CREEK)[27]

Marriage

There was considerable diversity in marriage customs but the essential feature of most marriage ceremonies was the consent of the girl's parents and the presentation of gifts to them.

Little, however, could compare with the complexity of the Kwakiutl marriage customs. Here, a man purchased both his wife and the privileges and rank of her family. When children came along, the wife's father surrendered all these privileges to them; however, with that debt redeemed, the husband then had again to make payment to his wife's family or the marriage would be annulled.[28]

Symbols were important in the Indian world and even the decoration on footwear could have significance. These Nez Perce buckskin and beaded moccasins (above) have floral patterns typical of the Plateau, patterns which may have been based on those originating in the east. The patterns are probably purely decorative; they could, however, make some reference to the powers believed to reside in the flora and fauna of the natural world.

The family unit was not complete without children and the coming of a baby into the world was a time to pray for its health and virtue
The Seminole family round this traditional fire (above) – the logs are fed into the fire as they are used – are all dressed in their distinctive clothing the colors of which (red, yellow, black and white) are significant in the area's medicine rituals. These two Navajo babies (above right) are swaddled in traditional rugs and blankets. A ceremony was held after their first laugh at which food was given away and following which the child was allowed possessions, usually beginning with jewelry.

While polygamy was relatively common among the Plains tribes and the younger sisters of the first wife were viewed as potential wives of the husband, polygamy was actually forbidden by the Iroquois and economic factors – it took a really expert hunter or wealthy man to support more than one wife – largely dictated the predominance of monogamy throughout most of North America.

If a marriage broke down, the wife generally returned to her parents and the children remained with her; both could remarry if they so desired.

The Family

In marriage, each partner had a definite sphere of responsibility and duty. Duties, however, varied considerably throughout the various cultural areas. Thus, among the largely horticultural and pastoral Zuni of the Southwest, the gardens were cultivated and owned by the women but the man was largely responsible for transportation of the produce. This contrasts markedly with the Plains tribes where, after the buffalo hunt, it was the women who butchered the meat and subsequently distributed it according to family needs.

The Child

Without question, the North American Indian had an intense love for their children and they bestowed upon them the fullest expression of affection and solicitude; the Teton Sioux, Higheagle, summed up a widespread attitude when he stated: 'It is strictly believed and understood by the Sioux that a child is the greatest gift from *Wakantanka*, in response to many devout prayers, sacrifices, and promises. Therefore, the child is considered "sent by *Wakantanka*", through some element – namely, the element of human being'.[29]

Contraception

Attempts at limiting family size were widely practiced either through sexual restrictions or by use of concoctions of some plant infusion, even burnt seashells in water.[30] Fairly widespread,

however, was a recognition of the link between conception and lactation. Typical is the observation of the Gros Ventre lady, Coming Daylight, 'The old-timers used to say that if a woman took good care of her children and kept them close to her, her family would not increase so rapidly'. Other Gros Ventre informants also referred to the use of oral contraceptives: 'lots of women took medicine. There are roots for that (contraception)'. It was also believed that it was possible for a man to take contraceptive medicine; one man who was known to take this was cited and none of his wives had children. Unfortunately, he gave his adopted son 'the medicine to drink and made the young man exceedingly unhappy, because he was very fond of children and none of his wives had any'.[31]

The Midwife

The Chippewa had midwives, *gataniwikwe*, who usually attended the mother at birth, but in many cultural areas it was the woman's mother, sister or other near relative. Medicine men and women were only called in if the labor was unusually hard and it appeared that the mother would not survive. It was not customary for any man, not even the husband, to be present at the birth: 'No; men had better stay away if they know what's good for them' observed one Chippewa informant![32]

Twins or Triplets

Twins or triplets were not generally desired since it was feared that the mother would die giving them birth. There was, almost universally, some awe associated with multiple births, although it was reported of the Arapaho that it was not 'institutional to ascribe supernatural power to twins',[33] and while one Chippewa informant said 'You know the Indians were scared when twins were born; they honored them as spirits . . . No supernatural powers, however, were ascribed to them'.[34] Nevertheless, there is some evidence which suggests that some tribes of the Oregon region and Northwest Coast did regard twins as

possessing strange powers, and tribes such as the Central Coast Salish, Quileute and Nootka might subject both parents and infants to prohibitions – such as remote isolation – for up to four years.[35]

The Navel Amulet

A custom, most highly developed among the Woodland, Plains and Plateau tribes, was that of saving the navel cord which was then used as an amulet. When thoroughly dry, it was generally rolled into a small coil and then wrapped in sage or sweetgrass. A small buckskin case, often beautifully beaded and some 4-6in (10-15cm) in length, enclosed the precious amulet, which was then attached to the outside of the cradle. This custom is obviously of ancient origin. It was described by George Catlin when he visited the Eastern Sioux in the vicinity of Fort Snelling in 1832. He said that it was suspended 'before the child's face, as its protector' and to ensure 'long life'.[36]

The navel cord was generally kept during the life of its owner; it was considered that saving it through childhood insured that girls and boys would

This double umbilical cord amulet (below) belonged to Crow twins and was tied to the cradle. A lizard signified swiftness, a turtle longevity.
Many such amulets were acquired from the Indians during the reservation period, sold by people whose morale was at a low ebb. Even so, the cord was always removed and buried and the buckskin of the amulet was resewn. Among the Apache the cord was often carried by the mother and if she lost it, it was said her child might die.

19

grow up to be women and men. They, therefore, became precious lifelong protective amulets to their owners and were generally buried with them.

Naming

While a child was generally named at birth or within a few days, it often being bestowed by a grandparent, that name was generally discarded as the girl or boy grew up for one of more important significance. Among the Hopi, it was traditional for the infant, when some 20 days old, to be dedicated to the sun, generally with considerable ceremonial and it was at this time that the name was given.[37]

The naming of a wealthy man's offspring among the Salish tribes of the Northwest Coast was frequently accompanied by a great celebration of feasting and gift-giving and a much respected elder was invited to announce publicly the names given.

Almost universally there were no family names[38] and when reaching adolescence or as adults, both men and women not uncommonly changed their names perhaps after the recovery from a serious illness, on the death of a much loved member of the family or more commonly after some unusual experience or deed. Thus, a Pawnee – and this is true of most Plains tribes – 'was permitted to take a new name only after the performance of an act indicative of great ability or strength of character' it being done 'during a public ceremonial'.[39]

Translation of Indian names has often led to gross distortion and sometimes outlandish misconceptions. Thus *Hajo Chito*, the name of an influential Creek leader, was officially rendered as 'Crazy Snake' when in fact *Hajo* was an ancient Creek war title signifying 'recklessly brave' and thus corrupted in translation to 'crazy'. A dire misconception also arose when the name of a Haida chief was rendered as 'Unable-to-buy' suggesting poverty status – in fact, it commemorated an occasion when a rival headman had insufficient wealth to purchase a much valued

copper which the Haida chief had to sell! Thus, even when translated correctly, an Indian name could convey a sentiment quite the reverse of its true connotation.[40]

Cradles and Cradle Types

Most cultural areas utilized a cradle although there were some notable exceptions to this. In the Arctic region, for example, where extreme cold prevailed, cradles were not used, the infant being carried within the hood of the mother's parka and the Mackenzie River tribes of the Subarctic region contained the baby in a bag of moss. In the warmer regions near or south of the Mexican border, frames and boards were not universal but the infant, generally wearing little clothing, was in various ways attached to the mother and borne on her hip, not infrequently resting in a hammock-like swing.

The country between these extremes of arctic and arid desert was the home of the cradle, the

style of which varied markedly from one cultural area to the next. Everywhere, however, the cradle was considered not only a bed but also a baby carriage and an infant generally utilized the cradle for at least one year. These cradles not only physically protected the child but also, by means of symbolic embellishments and use of carefully selected materials, ensured the total well-being of the child. Thus, Navajo cradles made in the Window Rock region of northern Arizona were traditionally made of two narrow cedar, piñon or pine boards with pointed upper ends and tied together so forming a backboard to which was added a hoop as a head protector and a foot board. The wood was traditionally taken from the eastern side of a secluded tree and which had not been damaged by the wind, struck by lightning, rubbed against by a bear or cut before the infant's death. The Navajo viewed the cradle itself as a microcosm of their universe which incorporated elements of the sky, the earth and the four sacred mountains so important in the mythology and religious teachings of the tribe.

Among the Pueblo, cradles were considered family heirlooms and were handed down from one generation to the next, the number of children they had carried being indicated by a series of notches cut in the frame. While the style varied from one pueblo to another, they did share several traits, such as making the cradleboard wood from a tree which had been struck by lightning,[41] generally making the faceguard staves of cedar (said to represent the rainbow), and cutting the upper edge of the board to give teeth-like slots which were symbolic of rain.[42]

In contrast to the Pueblan tradition of the cradle being a sacred family heirloom, those of the nomadic Plains tribes were generally made under the guidance of an experienced and much respected woman. They too were replete in symbolism which emphasized the world view of the tribe. Thus in the case of the Arapaho a distinct form of quilled rosette or trapezoid element was sewn on the hood of the cover, a style which was perpetuated 'well into the reservation period'.[43]

This superb Kiowa cradle (left) consists of a lattice of flat boards to which the carrying bag is tied or lashed. Note the Morning Star (top center), probably a protection for the child. The method of construction was similar to that of a number of other tribes from the central and southern Plains. The principal difference lay in the style of decoration of the beadwork, color and design often enabling the identification of a particular tribe.

Among the Plains tribes brothers and sisters grew up with strong bonds of kinship and as they grew older the brother often took on a protective role – such as among the Arapaho where the eldest brother traditionally gave advice as to his sister's conduct and gave consent to her marriage. At puberty, brothers and sisters no longer spoke to one another unless it was absolutely necessary and then only in a quiet, respectful way.

Several early fieldworkers reported that the hood had multiple symbolism: 'the sun, also the crown of the child's head, and its intelligence'.[44] Additionally, it was said to represent a tent ornament signifying that when the child had grown up he or she would have a tent, while four quilled pendants represented, among other things, the four old men important in mythology and the four periods of life.[45]

Only during a journey, while being carried about or at night was it laced in this microcosm of the Indians' universe and which embodied so much loving care and honor to the new-born child – which was a universal trait of the North American Indian.

If a child died at a helpless age, the intense grief of the mother and family caused the cradle to be thrown away, such as among the Walapai and various Tonto groups of the interior of Arizona. The Navajo and Apache on the other hand, burned, broke up or placed it on the child's grave, while the Kiowa and ancient cliff-dwellers

This Blackfeet woman (above) is wearing a distinctive dress that helps to identify her tribe, but she carries on her back a beautiful cradle (note the similarity to that on page 13) that is probably Cheyenne and that she has presumably acquired as a result of intertribal trade during the reservation period when this photograph was taken.

of New Mexico, Arizona and Colorado, buried it with the dead infant, who was laced up inside as in life.[46] Symbolic protection from death – coupled with a wisp of humor – was the custom of the Potawatomi and other tribes of Wisconsin, who traditionally cut one or two holes in the soles of the baby's moccasins. The rationale for this was that if an evil spirit asks the baby to go on a journey with him (to death), the baby can say 'I can't go with you; I have holes in my moccasins'.[47]

Childlife

As with all peoples, American Indian children delighted in imitating the occupations of their elders and children of both sexes had various toys and games. The boys practiced marksmanship, hunting, fishing, riding and the use of the bow or harpoon, but stilts, slings, tops, various ball games, forfeit plays (such as breath holding), 'catching', making 'cat's cradles', 'hunt the button', darts and not least, in warm weather, swimming, were all popular with both girls and boys. Girls were also inclined to dolls and 'playing house'. Some 'play' was of a more serious nature, as, for example, among the Hopi and Zuni where small wooden figures – *kachinas* – traditionally carved from the root of the cottonwood tree, were distributed as gifts from the masked dancers who appeared in the villages during the various ceremonials which generally began at the time of the winter solstice and ended late in July.[48] The *kachinas* not only impressed the sacred traditions in a tangible form, but as a pastime for children gave them religious training to enable them to learn 'the characteristics and names of over two hundred individual kachinas which they will see during their lifetime'.[49]

Puberty

Among the Plains tribes, the ceremonial piercing of the girl's ears for the insertion of decorative pendants, was a public announcement that she had reached puberty and was not infrequently accompanied by some ceremonial. Such an important event in the life of a Cheyenne girl has been

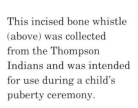

well-reported on by the anthropologist, George Bird Grinnell, who recorded that it was the custom among well-to-do people for the father of the girl to announce publicly from the lodge door what had happened 'and as an evidence of his satisfaction to give away a horse'.[50] The Cheyenne girl then unbraided her hair and bathed, and afterwards older women painted her whole body with red paint. Then, with a robe about her naked body, she sat near the fire, a coal was now removed from it and sweetgrass, juniper needles and white sage sprinkled on the burning ember. The girl now bent forward over it so that the smoke rising from the incense was confined and passed over her whole body. Then, accompanied by her grandmother, she left the family lodge and went into a specially erected small one where 'she remained for four days'.[51] Everything possessing a sacred character – medicine bundles, shields, headdresses – was kept well away from the girl; young men were prevented from eating or drinking from any pot used by her; one who did so would expect to be wounded in his next fight.[52]

Such practices, with various associated obligations and taboos, were found throughout most of the cultural areas, for it was widely believed that the supernatural powers were especially offended by menstrual blood. Thus, among the Tlingit, the fear of offending the fish spirits prohibited menstruants from approaching the fish streams,[53] and

a Haida girl was forbidden to go down to the beach at low tide or to cross a small stream. The Alaskan Eskimo were also fearful that the close proximity of a girl during her first menstruation, would affect their hunting weapons and that even shamans would lose their powers.[54] The period of isolation and fast, however, generally ended with a feast and public ceremonial, acknowledging that the girl was now of marriageable status. It was often at this time that the girl's face was tattooed, the operation usually being carried out by an older relative.[55]

While less precisely connected with the period of puberty, teenage boys also experienced rites of passage to adulthood. Thus, the end of childhood for the North Alaskan Eskimo boy was signaled by the piercing of the lower lip for labrets. The man who performed the painful operation was known for his skill in doing it quickly and efficiently; it was done by putting a piece of wood inside the mouth and then a chisel-like knife of stone was driven down through the flesh just under each corner of the mouth. The blood was wiped away and the wounds washed with urine which was 'taken into the mouth and expelled through the cuts'.[56] The labrets were then introduced. These were of three kinds, the one which was worn first and referred to as a *tuutak* was only an inch or less in diameter and was generally

This incised bone whistle (above) was collected from the Thompson Indians and was intended for use during a child's puberty ceremony.

These children (left) are playing with their miniature *tipis* as both a pastime and a practical way of becoming familiar with the *tipi's* structure, erection and maintenance – essential knowledge for the life ahead of them.

of wood or bone. As the individual became more successful and wealthy, however, the *tuutak* was replaced by a *simmeak* of an oblong shape some 1 1/2-2in (5cm) in length; the most coveted, however, was the *anmaloak* which was round, 2 1/2in (6cm) in diameter and only worn by men of high rank. Donning labrets was a sign that childhood and adolescence were passed and the wearer was free to find sexual partners and to marry.

Said to depict the male and female sexual organs, the handles of this cutting tool and knife (right) are carved from red (catlinite) stone. Collected from the Winnebago, these items were used as puberty instruments, the objects attached to the sheath being symbols of fertility and good luck.

Many tribes celebrated a girl's coming of age with her first menstruation and subsequently various customs were observed. Thus among the Winnebago a menstruating woman retired to a small lodge for the duration of her period. She was advised to sit and not look out during daylight; at night meals were served to her with special utensils so that people did not become 'infected'.

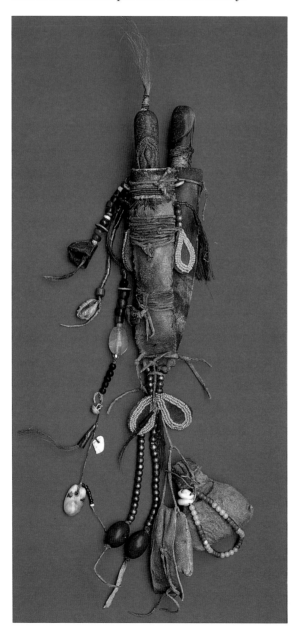

Early observers in the eastern part of North America have reported on the very severe tests used to determine which of the youths might make worthy candidates for admission to the ranks of great men of the nation. Of these, and among the earliest recorded (circa 1600) was that of the *Huskanaw* of the Virginian Algonquians – but which was also associated with the Virginia and North Carolina Siouans. *Huskanaw* is an Algonquian word which is said to mean, 'he has a new body' referring to a youth who had reached the age of puberty. Although there were variations, the major element of the ceremonial was for the young men to be confined in an isolated enclosure for several months during which time they were given a concoction made from roots which, as one early observer reported, drove them 'stark staring mad'. As a result of this treatment, the young men were supposed to forget – or at least pretend to forget – everything in their past, their parents, wealth, tongue etc., and to learn 'All things perfectly over again'.[57] One brutal part of their test was the pretended rescue of children placed at the foot of a tree and guarded by a lane of grown warriors armed with a baton made of reeds bound together. The youths had to run through the lane in turn to bring back a child and 'as he ran the guards rained unmerciful blows upon his body with which he protected the child'. In turn, the children were 'cast on a heap in a valley, as dead'.[58]

The Vision Quest

Widespread was the practice of the vision quest which was particularly important to the Plains, Prairie, Basin, Plateau and some Northwest Coast tribes at the time of puberty for a youth. In this, the youth made a solitary fast and vigil to obtain communication with his medicine or guardian spirit.[59] Generally, the fast lasted some four days when through dreams or visions, 'knowledge' was secured in a visitation by one or more spirits, one of which became his guardian spirit to help and protect him throughout his life. It was generally conceded that this was one of the most important things in life that could happen to a person and individuals who did not receive spiritual guardians through dreams or visions were sometimes considered less successful in their lives. Coast Salish described these spirits as having the appearance of animals or humanlike beings, but sometimes plants, artifacts and natural phenomena 'were also identified as sources of power'.[60] What was seen, often deter-mined the nature of a particular power acquired and was culturally biased; thus, the Western Shoshoni – who adopted much of the Plains Indian war complex in the 19th century – inter-preted the dreaming of a wolf as the source of war power. Previously, however, at a time when their culture was similar to that of most Great Basin tribes – non-aggressive – it represented the acqui-sition of the cunning of the wolf in the hunt.[61]

Indians all shared a faith in personal spirit guides which granted 'medicine' and power to the individual. Howard Terpning's painting Cheyenne Vision Seekers shows a group seeking a sign to avert a crisis. Normally a vision was sought alone at a place of religious significance or the site of a great historic event. The vision seeker fasted, prayed and chanted for a prescribed number of days and nights in the hope of receiving a visit from a spirit guide who would offer a direction to follow in life or a course of action to take.

KNOWLEDGE

'Almost every evening a myth, or a true story of some deed done in the past, was narrated by one of the parents or grandparents, while the boy listened with parted lips and glistening eyes...'

CHARLES EASTMAN (OHIYESA, SIOUX) [1]

A VARIETY OF METHODS was used by the North American Indians in their daily lives to document notable events in their history, as well as traditions, ceremonial and song, and to record transactions at the tribal or individual level.

These important memory aids – the written texts of Native Americans and imbedded in the eons of time – employed a variety of ingenious signs and symbols which differed markedly in both design and complexity. Among these were the ancient bark records of the Ojibwa and Delaware, the belts of wampum of the Iroquois, the painted pictographs on hide of the Plains tribes, engraved ivory or bone of the Eskimo, carved totem poles of the tribes of the Northwest Coast and the colored dry-paintings of such tribes as the Navajo in the Southwest . . . to name but a few. Later, came the ingenious Cherokee alphabet invented by Sequoya and which gave rise to the publication of a Cherokee newspaper in 1828, while the Cree alphabet – albeit developed in conjunction with missionaries – led to an almost universal language of the Subarctic region from the late-19th century onwards.

Oral History

In the 17th century memoirs of John Lederer, who traveled to the Pamunkey Indians – an Algonquian-speaking tribe of the Virginia tidewater area – reference is made to the 'matters concern(ing) the manners by which these people make up for their lack of letters to recall memorable matters'. The first of these was by songs 'which they learn in their youth and which they sing on the days of their festivals or new moons. These songs contain the mysteries of their religion and the great deeds of their ancestors'; additionally, Lederer made reference to the maintenance of tribal traditions 'delivered in long tales from father to son, which being children they are made to learn by rote'.[2]

More than 200 years later, in 1905, Seger recounted the importance of similar oral records for the Cheyenne, also an Algonquian tribe, but a people of the western Plains in the very heartland of North America: 'their history . . . has been handed down by word of mouth from generation to generation'. Seger's informant told him, the Cheyennes 'planted corn before they hunted buffalo'. The Cheyenne historian then said,

'I am of those who are appointed to keep (the history of the tribe), each one is required to make a vow and promise to the Great Spirit that he will never tell it as a story and will not tell it except in the presence of two others who are appointed to tell it and they must agree to every word as it is told, before the one who is telling it can go on'.[3]

Recording Time and Events

Among the simplest methods of recording time, was the employment of knotted cords or threaded

The transmission of knowledge was achieved most frequently by the oral tradition of story-telling and so on. Another method was the use of pictures or symbols to record the important events of the year or season. Here (main picture) a Lakota artist, Sam Kills Two (also known as Beads), is painting the so-called Big Missouri Winter Count that covers 1796 to 1926. The incised shell gorget (above left) refers to Mississippian belief. It is divided into four parts representing the four world quarters, each guarded by a crested woodpecker (symbol of war). The four quarters encircle a central disc that is the sun, in turn marked with a cross to symbolize the sacred fire kept burning continously. The Southwest's Navajo were expert silverworkers (right and far left) who used a system of dry-paintings in their religious and healing rituals, each of which was a highly complex design committed to memory.

This calendar stick (above) contains a Pima Indian's record of each year's events from 1833 to 1902. The notches represent a span of time, probably a year based on the annual harvest of the cactus. The mnemonic symbols relate the particular events concerned. Such sticks could be read by touch as well as sight and are just one example of an ingenious variety created by Native Americans.

Powhatan's Mantle (above right) is among the oldest surviving examples of North American Indian art. The animals either side of the human figure are somewhat stylized and therefore experts cannot be certain whether they are depictions of actual animals of the region or mythical composites. The former seems more likely, perhaps a white-tailed deer and a mountain lion. Although there has been much speculation as to whom this once belonged it is known that the puma and a large anthropoid were two of four protective images guarding Powhatan's treasure house in Orapakes.

beads or shells, which in various forms had intercontinental distribution.[4] Bourke, for example, in the 1880s, described the use of threaded beads by his Apache scouts for keeping records of the time of their absence on campaign and drew similar parallels to their employment by the Aztecs and Peruvian peoples,[5] and Jesuit priests, while at a council in a Huron town in 1653, reported that strings of shell beads were used to record such events and sentiments as the massacre of warriors and the long-standing bitterness between the French and Huron.[6]

The use of carved, painted or notched sticks for numeration and recording events was also widespread. Thus, the Shoshoni and Hidatsa tallied the number of days during which they journeyed from one place to another by cutting lines on sticks, while the Zuni incised the edges of small sticks to represent days and months.[7] More specialized was the use of the war post by Iroquois chiefs for documenting great events and keeping a chronology of them. The method was clearly effective and well-understood, as one close observer of the Iroquois recorded, 'by placing such significant hireoglyphics (sic) in so conspicuous a situation, they are enabled to ascertain with great certainty the time and circumstance of past events'.[8]

On a more personal level, war clubs and bows were frequently engraved with lines and pictographic figures recording successful war exploits. The custom was widely used, particularly in the Northeast by such tribes as the Mohawk, Onondaga, and other Iroquoian groups.[9] It was also recorded as in common use (circa 1680) among the Algonquian-speaking groups of Virginia's tidewater area, such as the six tribes in the powerful Powhatan confederacy.[10]

Early Mnemonic Records

More complex both in fabrication and the message contained, was the use of mnemonic records on hides, which we know date back to at least 1638, an example of which is now preserved in the collections of the Ashmolean Museum in Oxford and popularly described as 'Powhatan's Mantle'. It consists of four tanned skins of the white-tailed deer embellished with elaborate shell beadwork depicting a standing human figure flanked by two upright quadrupeds and surrounded by 34 discs.

The 'mantle' has been compared with the Plains Indian buffalo robe which has been well-documented for the 19th century,[11] the size, approximately 7$\frac{1}{2}$ft x 5ft (2.35m x 1.6m), being comparable to such robes. However, the manner of wearing required the ornamentation to run horizontally while the designs on the Powhatan 'mantle' are vertical. It thus seems more likely that the 'mantle' actually came from one of the *quioccosans* or 'temples' which were to be found in every one of the Powhatan villages and, perhaps not surprisingly since religion is so important to all human beings, is probably a record relating to the religious aspects of the tribe. The temples were furnished with carved images of *Okee* or *Okeus* who 'was responsible for all the evil in the world'.[12] Additionally, there were all 'kinds of Treasure, as skinnes, copper, pearle, and beades' as well as decorated skins.[13]

Early observers also reported that the Powhatan Indians had a great reverence for the sun as well as for the forces of nature and animals. Thus, the images worked on this hide – the earliest in existence – were records of some of the powerful and important figures of the Powhatan's universe – *Okee*, puma, deer and sun, the last of which we can almost certainly equate to the great god, *Atone*[14] who was responsible for all the good in the lives of the early Algonquian and Siouan peoples of the eastern seaboard region.[15]

Associated with these early religious records, were 'winter counts' which several generations later particularly 1870 onwards – were to be firmly linked with the Plains tribes such as the Sioux and Kiowa (see pages 36-37). The explorer, John Lederer, who traveled to the Pamunkey village of Pommaeomek in 1670 referred to their mnemonic devices for recording events. These, he said, were hieroglyphic wheels which the Pamunkey referred to as *Sag Ko Ho K.Quiacosough*, meaning the 'memory of the gods'. The wheels were described as of 60 sections, each of which represented one year 'as if they had wished to mark the age of sixty years which is ordinarily the span of a man's life'. These 'wheels' were painted on skins and kept in the sacred temples (referred to earlier) and in each section they marked the important events which had happened during one year by a hieroglyphic figure. Thus, the first arrival of Europeans was depicted by a swan expelling smoke and fire from its beak, the whiteness of the plumage of this bird and the water on which it was always depicted, Lederer reported, 'denoted the whiteness of the face of the Europeans and their arrival in Virginia from the sea, and they had made the smoke and fire in the beak of that bird to signify the firearms used by the Europeans'.[16]

The *Walam Olum*

There are some parallels here to the Lenni Lenape or Delaware Indians' pictographic account of their history in the so-called *Walam Olum*, a name which signifies a 'red painted score or tally'. These were a set of flat, wooden tablets with incised pictographs infilled with red paint; their origin was preserved in the oral lore of the tribe. The anthropologist Harrington reported on their use just as a tribal sage may have explained it:

'One time, long ago, when our ancestors resided in the North, there lived a man who believed that the story of our people should never be forgotten. Knowing that men are, by nature, forgetful, he tried to plan some way to make them remember. Finally, it is said, a method of doing this was revealed to him in a dream ... he was instructed to prepare flat, wooden tablets and to paint upon them pictures in red which would call to mind the things he wished to remember. To begin

The Plains warriors spent a great deal of time recording things on animal hides and other objects – most of all they recorded their war exploits or pictorial biographies. Once this activity was denied them after confinement to the reservations, men with time on their hands produced even more such drawings. Winter counts, although wholly traditional, were one example of this and were produced on hide, paper and muslin sheeting. This count (left) is on paper and thus breaks with tribal tradition which was oral. It was produced by Bull Plume, a *Siksika* Blackfeet man.

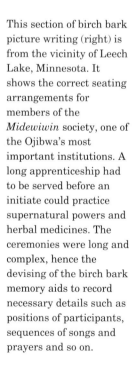

This section of birch bark picture writing (right) is from the vicinity of Leech Lake, Minnesota. It shows the correct seating arrangements for members of the *Midewiwin* society, one of the Ojibwa's most important institutions. A long apprenticeship had to be served before an initiate could practice supernatural powers and herbal medicines. The ceremonies were long and complex, hence the devising of the birch bark memory aids to record necessary details such as positions of participants, sequences of songs and prayers and so on.

with, he painted the stories of the first days of the world as they were told by the old men of his time; then, he painted pictures to represent important things as they happened. On his death the tablets and the work were carried on by his family until the present day . . . they tell the story of our Lenape tribe: whence we came and how we arrived in this country where we live today. Only the owner and his helper know just what the pictures mean, and they carry the tablets around from village to village and recite the story. Each picture reminds the owner of one part of it, so he cannot forget'.[17]

These complex memory aids, it has been suggested, lend themselves to a depth of interpretation rivaling that of the Hebrew characters which were used in the writing of the Old Testament and begin with a Genesis superior to that reported from the first ages of Christianity; the *Walam Olum* can thus be likened to the text of a Lenape (Delaware) Bible, the initial verses and symbols describing the origin of order and harmony combined in the universe and, as described, their later history.[18] Of particular interest is that one of the pictographs, as with the Pamunkey's 'memory of the gods' discussed earlier, documents the arrival of the white man in a large ship surmounted by a cross and which undoubtedly refers to the extensive contacts on the Atlantic seaboard to the east in the late-15th century.[19]

The Lenape were regarded as a senior nation by such tribes as the Huron and Creek. With the increasing white intrusion, their role as arbitrators and diplomats became particularly important and many of their activities in this sphere are recorded on the *Walam Olum*.[20]

The Ojibwa *Midewiwin* Records

Closely associated with the pictographs exhibited on the Lenape *Walam Olum*, were those employed by the Ojibwa and exemplified in the repertoire of 'literary' records in the form of birch bark scrolls which were used by *Midewiwin* or

'Grand Medicine Society' members to document that complex ceremonial. The *Midewiwin* was very much part of the daily life of the Ojibwa and other central Algonquian groups as its members were considered 'repositories of tribal traditions, origins, and migrations integrated in *systems* of myth and legend'.[21]

These records or charts were considered sacred and never exposed to public gaze and only after an accepted candidate had both paid his entrance fee, gone through fastings and made offerings, was he allowed to view them. One chart was over 7ft (2m) in length and some 18in (46cm) wide and made of five pieces of birch bark carefully stitched together with strands of basswood. Formerly the property of a principal Ojibwa shaman called *Badasan,* it dated from 1825 and documents Ojibwa religion, recording not only the traditional history of the origin of the *Midewiwin* and Ojibwa migrations, but also the position of various spiritual guardians and 'the

order of procedure in study and progress of the candidate'.[22]

Reference is also made to *Minabozho*, 'Great Rabbit', the messenger of *Dzhe Manido*, the 'Good Spirit', who by his good offices ensured continued life and good things which were necessary for both health and subsistence. It was *Minabozho* who instructed Otter, adopted as one of the sacred *manidos*, 'spirits', in the mysteries of the *Midewiwin* and who gave to the society the sacred rattle, drum and tobacco which was used in the *Mide* ceremonials.

Much of the *Mide* ceremonials were public, the rituals, dances and feasts lasting up to eight days.[23] Often the application to join was the result of a dream but in recent years even babies who were, or had been, ill, could be inducted into the society – which although a break from tradition, is a feature common to many such movements where there is a 'transmutation of ancient ritual practices and beliefs to new ideological and ritual contexts'.[24]

In the case of the Ojibwa, the stress of reservation conditions which caused the progressive breakdown of the tribe, led to a far greater emphasis on curing and prayers for health and regeneration during the *Midewiwin* ceremonials.

Deciphering Pictographs

The evidence indicates that pictograph images of the type described were far more intelligible to the people who produced them than to the uninitiated and that communication crossed linguistic barriers, especially when read in a particular context. Thus, in 1820, when Governor Lewis Cass traveled to the region of the mouth of the St. Peter's River, not far from present-day St. Paul, he noted that the members of an Ojibwa party who were on a peace mission to the Santee(?) Sioux, had no difficulty in deciphering an extensive pictograph message delivered from the Sioux. This was on a 'piece of birch bark, made flat by fastening between two sticks at each end and about 18 inches long by 2 broad'. A similar message had been sent earlier by the Ojibwa to the Santee and this was their reply:

'The proposition had been examined and discussed in the Sioux villages and the bark contained their answer. The Ojibwa explained to us with great facility the intention of the Sioux . . . (and) the effect of the discovery of the bark upon the minds of the Ojibwas was visible and immediate'.[25]

Messages and symbols etched in stone can date from many thousands of years. Their contemporary purpose was to invoke spiritual power, display warnings and messages, and so on. Their precise meanings were often lost on those not familiar with the intricate symbols being used, that most are a mystery to us today should not come as a surprise. Those seen here are carved into rocks at Sproat Lake, Canada, (left) and Dry Creek Ford, Colorado, (below). Typically, they show strange human forms and animal representations, as well as abstract designs and curious geometrical markings.

The Sealing of Treaties – the Wampum Belt

The term wampum derives from an eastern Algonquian word meaning 'white strings (of shell beads)'. This wampum belt (above) consists of eight rows of white whelk shell and purple clam shell beads aligned between nine warps of leather cord on wefts of vegetable fiber, as can be seen where the original beads are missing. The beads were drilled in order to be strung, production increasing greatly once metal drills were introduced by Europeans.

Wampum was used in bracelets, collars and caps, the patterns often being highly symbolic. It is in belt form – used as a mnemonic device in a ceremonial and political context – that most have survived. Hundreds were created to record negotiations and inter-ethnic relations following European settlement. Onondaga chief David John Sr. (right) is seen in 1910 holding wampum strings representing the Six Nations.

At the establishment of the League of the Iroquois, which probably took place in the middle of the 16th century, it was the Onondaga, the most centrally located of the five Iroquois tribes, who became the keepers of the League's archives. These were in the form of long sashes or belts made of white and purple cylindrical beads, a quarter of an inch (6.5mm) or slightly more in length.

The belts were used in sealing the pledges of a treaty between the Iroquois and other Indian nations and later between the Iroquois and Europeans. They were referred to by the Iroquois as *Kari hwa*, the 'authentic credential', or *gawenna*, 'the voice, the word, or the proposition'.[26] Wampum thus played a central role in the governing process of the sophisticated social and political organization of the Iroquois. A great mystical power was assigned to the beads which extended not only to the approval and documentation of council proceedings but vouched for the honesty of the speaker, gave great authority to his office and, in some circumstances, were used to ease sorrow.[27]

The custom was obviously of ancient origin, possibly initiated by Hiawatha, one of the founders of the League of the Iroquois and active around 1570; prior to this it seems probable that the sashes or belts were made of cut porcupine quills. Of interest is that the name Hiawatha is sometimes translated as 'seeker after wampum'.[28]

Kahkewaquonaby or 'Sacred Feathers', an Ojibwa leader,[29] described one belt which had been used in a treaty between the League of the Iroquois and the Ojibwa. The council fire was depicted as 'a beautiful white fish' signifying purity 'that all our hearts may be white toward each other'; a white deer denoted 'superiority' and adjacent symbols of a dish and ladles indicated an abundance of game and food. An eagle perched on a tall pine symbolized a watchfulness on all the council fires between the Iroquois and Ojibwas. The most dominant symbol, however, was that of the sun, by whom they swore that they would forever after observe the treaties made between the two parties.[30]

One of the longest of wampum belts, known as the Washington Covenant, is more than 6ft (2m) long and 5in (13cm) wide, and is traditionally thought to date from around 1790, made in order

32

to commemorate a covenant of peace between the 13 original colonies, under President George Washington, and the Iroquois confederacy.

To ensure accuracy, keepers of these sashes – the elders of the people – traditionally assembled periodically to rehearse the matters which were represented by the bead patterns. In particularly complex and important matters, the elders were charged with remembering only a portion of the record, thus ensuring that nothing of consequence was lost. Such was the archive of the Iroquois oral records supported by mnemonic devices and available to the people, which through their distinguished and trusted keepers, brought stability, meaning, and order to their daily lives.[31]

Heraldic Display and Social History

Underlining the nature of the social and political organization of the Northwest Coast tribes, were the carved cedar poles erected by the various Indian groups along the Pacific coast extending from Vancouver to Alaska. Often raised with much ceremonial during the time of the great feasts and giveaways – The Potlatch – one or more skilled sculptors were employed to carve emblems of mythical and real figures representing family crests, a record of events, or perhaps even the figure of someone who was ridiculed by the house owner. As one scholar in this field has observed of the Haida, whose gigantic totem poles dominated the Queen Charlotte Island village beaches in the 19th century,

'these great images equalled the power of any of the world's sculpture . . . their function was to proclaim the rank and social affiliation of the house owner and his wife, or to memorialize a deceased predecessor. The figures were crests or figures in the mythical adventures of lineage ancestors'.[32]

In going about their daily lives, the people recognized the significance of several different types of large carved wooden objects where totemism

It is one of the ironies of European settlement that the things they introduced sometimes created a native culture – such as the nomadic horsepeople of the Plains – or they strengthened and reaffirmed longstanding traditions while simultaneously eroding them by the very act of contact.
European trading ships supplied the Northwest Coast tribes with steel adzes and chisels which enabled them to work with wood on a scale previously unimaginable. It marked a period of proliferation of huge clan and crest poles. This pole (left) is known as the 'Hole in the Sky' pole and was used originally as a ceremonial entrance to Haidzemerhs' house in the Tsmishian village of Kitwancool. It contains crest and ancestor figures fused with mythical and semi-historical events. Haidzemerhs was a member of the Wild Rice clan in the Wolf division and wolves therefore feature prominently as the principal crest – atop the pole is the figure of Migrating Wolf.

Many objects were worn which carried family heraldic and clan crests and totemic figures. This item of headgear (right) is the wooden clan helmet, with copper inlays, of a Haida chief. The eight twined basketry rings added to the top denote each occasion that the chief sponsored a successful potlatch, clearly announcing that this particular chief was a wealthy man of some considerable status.

could be displayed: mortuary and house posts, memorial and house frontal poles. Mortuary poles were erected to hold the remains of a person of high rank such as a chief or shaman, the body or the ashes being contained in a compartment at the top of the pole which was a front board carved and painted with the personal emblem of the dead person.

While house posts – which constituted an integral part of the building and supported the main beams – were often carved and painted, it was the outside memorial and frontal poles which documented events, told ancestral legends and displayed the owner's clan crests for all to see. Thus, the early contacts of the Haida with the Russians in the mid-18th century,[33] were commemorated by a memorial post erected at Kasa-an, on Prince of Wales Island. The property of the Haida chief, *Skowal*, it stood at the back of his house as a ridicule or discredit pole. *Skowal* was represented by his eagle crest which surmounts a Russian making a pious gesture. Below are carved a winged angel and the Russian Orthodox priest, with folded arms, who had made a fruitless attempt to convert the chief and his people to a white man's religion.[34]

There were considerable variations in the tribal styles. Haida poles on the Queen Charlotte and Prince Edward Islands, for example, had carved figures which were highly detailed, clustered and generally square cut while the pole itself tended to taper towards the top. Tsimshian poles were similar but were generally somewhat slender, with less closely knit designs. It was probably with these two tribes that the use of distinctive and tall posts was first developed; certainly they were, in the middle to late-19th century, producers of the most elaborate and technically fine carved poles. The carved poles of the Tlingit, who lived to the north of the Haida and Tsimshian, combined features found in the style used by these latter tribes – sharply cut but relatively simple in design – while to the south among the Bella Coola, poles were short and broad with a distinctive taper and hollowed out

behind to a marked degree. Kwakiutl poles tended to be rather poor imitations of the Haida-Tsimshian although about 1890 a new style was developed which was characterized by bright complex painting, carefully adzed surfaces, carving in high relief and trimmed with wings made of thin boards, a style which also extended to the Coast Salish and Nootka who earlier made but limited use of the totem pole.

It was at the raising ceremonial that some of the meaning of the pole was explained by its owner to those assembled. However, the full meaning and 'archival' value of these various superb forms of artwork to tribal members, is still to be fully unraveled. In the 1940s, Claude Levi Strauss, building on the pioneering fieldwork of anthropologists such as Franz Boas and George

Emmons, suggested that Northwest Coast art, its cultural product, was a definite expression of that society's structure and held a deeper and more complex intellectual content than the totemic symbols suggested to outsiders.[35] For example, as one researcher has recently (and quite convincingly) demonstrated, an elaborate image previously identified as a 'hawk' is, in fact, a 'salmon' and instead of being a mere *noun*, actually refers to a complex process of cyclic regeneration so that the visual image is a *verb* in any message about transformation, evoking an elaborate and sophisticated thought process relating to the sacred and profane, seasons, birth, death and metamorphosis.[36] Thus, the totem pole in its various forms, as well as masks and other ceremonial regalia, acted as tangible and significant memory aids to the village at large. It documented history of both family and tribe, clan affiliations and made reference to involved and extensive myths and legends.[37]

Without a written language, ideas, emotions, and events, were recorded by complex and impressive artwork – 'image texts' – with discernable codes and messages[38] which conveyed subtle and diverse information to the populace that few outsiders could ever even begin to comprehend.[39]

Images of Ceremonial and Religion

The essential aspects of much traditional tribal thought, religious beliefs and mythology were recorded in the so-called dry-paintings of several tribes in the Southwest, such as the Navajo and Hopi, although the custom – generally less developed – was also found among the Plains tribes, such as the Cheyenne and Arapaho and even extended to the Blackfeet on the northern Plains.

Dry-painting reached its greatest development among the Navajo, who used larger and more elaborate designs than any other tribe. The pictures were made primarily in connection with religious ceremonials and not only represented various gods in their mythology but documented the sequence by ingenious – often conventionalized – representations of natural phenomena such as lightning, sunbeams, mountains, animals, plants and rainbows.

Historically, always guided by sacred myths and legends which related to the tribe's emergence from darkness to the present world, the Navajo incorporated into their ceremonials these complex dry-paintings as a type of holy altar.[40] Many of the ceremonials were associated with healing, since an important facet of the Navajo's world view was that illness was due to disharmony which had resulted by transgressions against one's own body and mind, the sick individual having failed to maintain harmony with the environment and perhaps infringed the ceremonial rules and practices. By prayer, concentration and then application of sacred pollen, the exact cause of the patient's illness was determined by the 'hand trembler' – so called because this diagnostician's hands trembled a particular way during the ceremonial. The nature of the movements identified the type of disharmony in the patient and so determined the subsequent 'sing', often referred to as a 'chant' or 'way', to effect the cure.

In preparation for the ceremonials, helpers were instructed to gather the necessary materials for the dry-paintings. Often collected in the still of

These two Navajo *hatalis* (below) are preparing a dry-painting ceremonial, a form of spiritual art that has evolved over many centuries into a highly complex form. There might be a thousand multicolored designs which need to appear in a single painting. The paintings form a major part of Navajo healing rituals, some of which take place over a nine-day period. Here, the pigments are being trickled in fine amounts onto a fresh bed of sand on the flooor of a traditional *hogan*. The patient will sit on the painting, facing east – the direction whence all Navajo blessings come. The supernatural powers will enter and, if pleased, make it their home and thus cure the patient. The sand is later disposed of ceremonially.

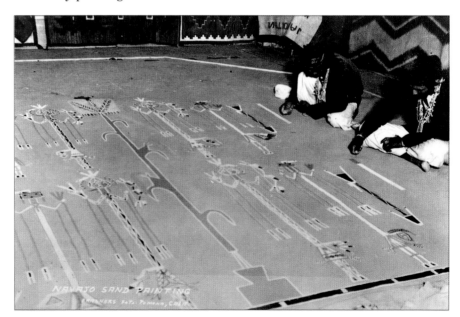

These tall *yei* figures are deities or invisible Earth Spirits of the Navajo. They often appear in dry-paintings but for many years it was taboo to weave them. Encouraged by white traders, however, some weavers were prepared to commit sacrilege and once it was seen that there was no supernatural retribution this form of weaving, based on sacred dry-paintings, caught on. This particular rug dates from about 1880, probably from the Shiprock region, and has a rainbow border and a sacred corn plant at its center.

the early morning, the materials included not only sand – perhaps with a specific instruction such that it should come from the bed of a straight-flowing stream – but various pollens, cattail, crushed flowers, charcoal and colored sandstone. All these vegetal plants and minerals were then pulverized and placed in trays of juniper bark. The fine consistency ensured smooth flow of material from the palm of the hand down through a channel between the thumb and forefinger. The pigments represented the five sacred colors of Navajo mythology – black, blue, white and yellow symbolized the four cardinal directions and red, the sunshine.

In a curing ritual, the patient is seated on the completed dry-painting and then parts of it are scattered on his or her body, the painting having first been strewn with sacred pollen or cornmeal to protect its curative powers. Now with poetic chants, the myths and associated deities are invoked, the medicine man relating the body of

the sick person to the body of the deity, head to head, hand to hand, foot to foot and mind to mind, so replacing the evil in the patient by all that is good in the dry-painting.[41]

Not all rituals were associated with the healing of one individual, thus the elaborate and lengthy ceremonial of the Nightway, which took place in the winter months, served to restore tribal health in body, mind and spirit, all of which fell to a low ebb in the long winter desert nights. The Blessingway, on the other hand, provided the Navajo people with their own 'rites of passage'. It refers to a most beloved and revered deity, 'Changing Woman', the mystery of reproduction and one who created the Navajo.[42]

Winter Counts

The ancient techniques of recording time and events referred to earlier for the Indians of Virginia – their hieroglyphic wheels which they call the 'memory of the gods' – was to be found two centuries later among the Plains Indians, particularly the Sioux and Kiowa, who produced calendric histories which were painted, at least traditionally, on tanned buffalo hides.[43]

In the Sioux calendars, sequence of years in calendrical form was correlated for each year with some notable event. They were generally referred to as a *waniyetu yawapi* or 'winter count' since 'winter' was designated as from the first snowfall through that winter, spring, summer and autumn until the first snowfall of the following year.[44]

As the 'keeper of the count' added the pictograph to the calendar, he would also compose a short phrase relating to the significance of the pictograph; the recording was considered a serious matter and as the keeper's memory began to fail with age, a younger man was trained to take over the responsibility. This new keeper, who often paid for the privilege, then rehearsed the verbal phrases using the pictograph figures as memory aids. 'From this skeletal framework the

keeper could expand the historical account, adding details and background information not indicated in either the pictograph or its accompanying phrase'.[45]

While the counts approximated to the function of histories in the English sense of the word, they were also important as calendars, keeping track of the sequential events in successive years. As one authority observed, 'The fact that a bizarre or unusual event . . . was often selected to mark a year rather than a seemingly more important occurrence of a less novel nature would indicate that this calendrical function of the counts was almost equal in importance to their function as historical records'. If an individual was not certain how old he was, 'having been told that he had been born in the winter "The stars showered down" (1833) the person would approach the keeper of the count and ask that official to point out this pictograph to him . . . he could then count the remaining pictographs on the near side of this event to learn his exact age'.[46] The falling stars pictograph is shown in the Winter Count kept by the Oglala, Cloud-Shield. This event is noted on most extant counts and refers to the spectacular meteor showers which were apparently visible throughout North America in December 1833 and acts as an 'index' in checking the chronological accuracy of a Plains Winter Count. Cloud-Shield's calendar covers the years 1775 to 1878 and records such events as military engagements, intertribal warfare as well as epidemics, ceremonialism, climate and various aspects of material culture. A similar count was kept by American Horse who stated in 1879 that 'his grandfather

began it, and that it (was) the production of his grandfather, his father and himself'.[47]

Likewise, with the Kiowa, one particularly important calendar having been made by *Dohasan* or 'Little Bluff' who was head chief of the tribe for more than 30 years.[48] This, according to the family, had been started in the early 1830s and was originally painted on hides which were renewed from time to time as they wore out from handling and age. The pictographs were arranged in a continuous spiral; winter was designated by an upright black bar indicating that the vegetation was then dead, while summer was represented by means of a figure of a medicine lodge – a time when such ceremonials took place.[49]

Kiowa calendars were seemingly more precise than the Sioux calendars since two pictorial devices identified each year, one representing the winter months, the other the summer. The *Dohasan* and other Kiowa calendars actually covered a most critical period in Kiowa history – approximately 1832-92.[50]

These tribal records were frequently brought out for discussion around the Kiowa campfires during the long winter nights 'to be exhibited and discussed in the circle of warriors about the tipi fire'. The signal for such a gathering took the form of an invitation to the camp members to 'come and smoke', shouted in a loud voice throughout the camp by the head man. Then the pipe was filled and passed around, each warrior in turn reciting the meaning of a particular pictograph which was then discussed by the assembled body of people.[51] 'Thus the history of the tribe is formulated and handed down'.[52]

The peoples of the Arctic region – especially the hunters – often recorded events and incidents on pieces of ivory. The carving of ivory has been taught there for 2,000 years. This tusk (above) shows a hunter's record of one of his seal-trapping expeditions, such scenes often being intended to honor the animal spirits and insure an abundance of game. Designs were incised with a sharp point – often jade in the early days – and the lines were then rubbd with charcoal mixed with grease. This tusk was collected in the Seward Peninsula in 1892 and is particularly valuable because of its colors which are rare on decorated tusks.

RECREATION AND PASTIMES

*'Only the foot could be used to move the ball toward
the goal. It required a great deal of speed and
dexterity on the part of the player.'*

STRACHEY (CIRCA 1612)[1]

ORAL 'LITERATURE', MUSIC, song and dance of the North American Indian reflected the diversity of their social structures, religious beliefs, customs and lifestyles. This diversity too was embedded in the wide variety of games, both of chance and dexterity, which not only developed the necessary skills for survival but frequently evoked the myth and powers of the tribal cultural heroes.

Story-telling

The winter solstice, when people were largely immobilized and tended to stay together, was marked by ceremonial gift exchanges, riddling and story-telling. While every adult possessed a store of practical knowledge such as weather lore, remedies for minor illnesses as well as genealogical and cosmological data and information on past historical events, there were others who were recognized as possessing additional specialized knowledge. These individuals had the ability to relate myths and legends or even to predict the future through such rituals as scapulimancy. Thus, during the long winter months, together with such activities as preparing pelts and hides, making, mending and embellishing clothing and weapons, there was much recounting of the traditional tales: then the older people passed on much of their knowledge to the young so teaching them many of the rules of social behavior, tribal traditions, religion, ethics and educational patterns.

A good raconteur was particularly appreciated and creative variation was generally condoned. Among the Chippewa, many elderly women were recognized as experts in this art and at least 'one old woman used to act out her stories, running around the fire and acting while she talked'.[2] Acting out some of these tales was a widespread practice. Thus, a Northwest Coast story-teller might raise his voice 'to a squeal as he imitated one character, growling, roaring or weeping for others (and) the hearers knew by heart the queer expressions which belonged to each . . . at certain points the hearers said something like amen to show they were awake'.[3] Some tribes repeated the speaker's last word or even a whole sentence which related to components so important to survival, such as 'Keep bad luck from the salmon' of the Coastal Salish.[4]

While basic traditions and lore were perpetuated, the fund of stories was constantly expanded by contacts with other tribes or whites – such as traders and missionaries.[5] Creation myths were common and these formed an important component in the story-teller's repertoire and generally reflected the atmosphere of a particular cultural area.[6] Other enduring tales involved historical events such as that of *Thanadelther* who first guided the English to the Chipewyan, while stories which emphasized the relationship of man to nature were extensive. In one set of such traditional tales, the Chipewyan are identified with the wolf, whose pattern of reliance and predation on the caribou 'is remarkably similar to the tradi-

Games provided a means of social interaction, entertainment, education and relaxation, as well as perhaps imparting skills necessary for hunting and so on. This hand game played by Paiutes (main picture) was photographed near Kanab, Utah, in 1872. There is a team on either side, the counters from each in the foreground. The two players of the team on the left are hiding the bones – one marked, one unmarked – while the other team tries to guess their positions. Some games were played seasonally when distant bands of a tribe met at camp. One such game was the Carrier version of ring and pole played between rival bands of the tribe's warriors. The ring (above left) was made of a bundle of twigs lashed together with strips of willow bark. Such activities kept warriors fit and better able to raid and count coup against their enemies.(A coup stick handle is seen here, right and far left.)

tional Chipewyan pattern (and) reincarnation as man or wolf may occur, often with extraordinary or miraculous powers . . .'.[7]

Many of the myths and legends were long, taking several hours to relate. Often they were replete with repeated phrases which the listeners were generally familiar with and responded to with an 'Ahh'. It is, however, reported for the Sauk and Fox of the prairies of Iowa, that they preferred short succinct tales,[8] and here it was not unusual for a story to come to an abrupt halt rather than have a proper ending: such phrases as 'that is the way they tell it' or 'that is as far as the story goes'.[9] In all this, children were generally allowed to sit by and listen in; sometimes, however, stories were told primarily for their amusement. Typical was a story told by an aged

Arapaho to Sister Inez Hilger some fifty years ago, who 'after a chuckle' related the following:

'A man went on the warpath. He was tired and came back. On the way home at night he saw a *tipi* in which a fire was glowing. It was a pretty sight. He walked up to it and found one woman there. She made a bed for him and he slept there. The next morning when he woke up, he saw a skeleton in rags above him. And he was in an old ragged *tipi*, too. The *tipi* he had seen the night before was a pretty *tipi*. – What he saw was probably like the burials of the Cheyenne, they bury in trees you know. – Well, this man never stopped again. He walked day and night until he got home'.[10]

Blackfeet Storyteller by Howard Terpning captures the sense of wonder and interest which a good story-teller can obtain from an audience, whether composed of children, adults, or both. Tales were told for amusement, instruction, as accounts of warrior exploits, or perhaps tribal legends relating the ancient ways and beliefs which should not be lost. Note the medicine bag hanging from the neck of the elder telling the story.

As discussed earlier, the use of pictographic records was widespread and these were resorted to in the rendition of the oral tales. One Chippewa girl reported that her father 'had birch bark with writing on it . . . young people were not allowed to look at it'. Her grandfather had a roll of birch bark 'there were only birds and animals marked on it . . . He said, 'I know what it means. I can read it'.[11]

While the Chippewa pictographic system of mnemonic records was well-developed and more nearly approached writing, the art of scapulimancy was somewhat different. The activity was an important component of Subarctic oral 'literature' evoking much discussion around the winter camp-fires; for here, the powers of both *Kitchi-Kitchi-Manitou* 'Great-Great Spirit' and *Maci-Manitou* 'Evil Spirit' as well as *Windigo* 'the cannibal' were evoked in the complexities of divinity relating to such things as life, success, sickness and luck.[12]

The practice of scapulimancy is ancient, sustained and widespread, particularly in the Subarctic. It was reported on by a missionary who stayed with the Montagnais in the winter of 1633-34 and **filmed** in a Montagnais camp on Goose Bay, Newfoundland, in the autumn of 1989.[13]

Music and Song

Music was an immense source of pleasure to the North American Indian and skills, according to their standards, were both appreciated and honored. Music to them, in its highest sense, according to one outstanding authority on the subject, 'is connected with power and with communication with the mysterious forces that control all human life (and) in that, even more than in the sound of the singing, lies the real difference between the music of the American Indian and that of our own race'.[14]

Thus, music was coextensive with tribal life; it was used in every public and religious ceremony as well as in each important facet of an individual's life. Music was generally considered to be the property of societies, clans or individuals and it followed a distinctive rhythm; accompaniment

was usually by rattles, flutes, whistle and drum.

Song Duels and Contests

Song duels were very much a characteristic of the Arctic region 'where each one strove to ridicule the adversary'.[15] The opponents met by appointment and sang sarcastic songs to each other; the one who created the most laughter among the assembled audience, was deemed to be the victor!

Dance very often accompanied music and song. This image painted by Karl Bodmer (below) depicts a Hidatsa dancer from the Crazy Dog Society. The headdress is made from magpie tail feathers with a crest of turkey tail feathers.

The tribes of California had a range of impressive dance ceremonies. These Yurok dancers (above) are wearing brightly colored woodpecker and bluebird feather headbands, intricate shell necklaces, and deerskin aprons. The men to the right are holding long basketry-type money purses. Such dances – sometimes lasting 10 days – were held to ward off disaster and to regenerate or renew the people and their world for the year ahead. The rich and beautiful objects were displayed in order to show the gods how worthy and industrious the people were. Woodpecker scalps in particular were difficult to obtain in large numbers, hence their use as an indicator of wealth and status.

Such contests served a very important social function, particularly among the East Greenland groups, as they prevented the development of open conflict. Thus, if an individual felt that his life was threatened 'he could save himself by challenging his opponent in song. One had to treat his opponent in a song duel as a beloved guest; a song duel was a celebration that everyone attended in his finest clothes'.[16]

Song contests found expression in other cultural areas and involved more than single individuals. Although generally in unison, women's voices were often high-pitched, at least an octave above the male singers particularly when urging warriors to take courage on the warpath. Plains Indian women's singing was described by one observer thus:

'Their shrill, metallic-voiced songs of encouragement urge on the departing war party to greater exertions, to braver deeds, and the same shrill voices give them praise and welcome on their return, and should any have fallen, for days their weird wild chanting fills the air of the camp with the great deeds of those who have been slain, and this honor is dearly prized by the savage heart'.[17]

Musical Proficiency

One particular characteristic of Chippewa singing – although it was certainly not exclusive to that tribe and occurred throughout the Woodlands and beyond – was the use of a vibrato, or wavering tone, generally regarded as a marked sign of musical proficiency while in the Drum Dance the women who accompanied the men's singing, produced a nasal, 'high-keyed humming by keeping their mouths closed and holding their noses partly shut with one hand'.[18]

Most ceremonial songs were an emotional appeal to the supernatural powers and their accuracy of rendering was considered essential to ensure that the appeal followed the correct path, otherwise evil consequences might follow.

Dream Songs

One vital component of American Indian music was the so-called 'dream song' which was common to most of the cultural areas. The songs were not composed but were said to come in a dream which to the Indian

'implies an acute awareness of something mysterious. Dreams and their songs may come . . . in natural sleep . . . but the first important dream comes to a young man in a fasting vigil. He is alone in some silent place, . . . his mind is passive, as he hopes for an impression to come to him from a mysterious source. The silence becomes vibrant, it becomes rhythmic, and a melody comes to his mind.'[19]

This is his 'dream song', his most individual possession. '. . . The Indian waited and listened for the mysterious power pervading all nature to speak to him in song (he) realized that he was part of nature – not akin to it'.[20]

Dream songs were sung in war dances, the name of the warrior being honored in this way, sometimes using a 'sacred language'. The use of a sacred language in song has been particularly well-documented for the Lakota[21], and touched on for the Mandan.[22] The idea was, however, widespread. Thus, Young Doctor, a Makah Indian from the Northwest Coast, related a dream in which the Southwest Wind appeared to him in the form of a man and sang a song, the words of which were unintelligible and which he termed 'wind language'.[23]

Other styles of sacred language were in the form of 'coded' statements, the meaning of which was only intelligible to the initiated, such as the songs associated with the Yaqui Deer Dance. These songs concerned the actions of various animals and the manifestations of nature; one translated to 'The bush is sitting under the tree and singing'. While 'singing' was the correct translation, in the context of the song it referred to the existence of a magical power, the bush sharing in the power 'that pervades the universe'.[24]

Often, an animal or bird appeared in a dream at the time the song was acquired. Among the Lakota, for example, a dream of a bear was par-

ticularly favored by those who wished to become a *pejuta wicasa* or 'medicine man', since the bear had good claws for digging herbs and could reveal certain materials which could be used in treating the sick.[25] The creature seen in the dream was frequently mentioned in the song and incorporated in the individual's name, thus *Tatanka-ohitika* or 'Brave Buffalo' said he had his first dream when he was 10 years old and he 'saw a buffalo'. Later he dreamed of elk and wolves and he recorded the songs received in these dreams.[26]

It was customary for an individual to carry or wear some article connected with his dream. Indeed, a song connected with the Sun Dance mentions the wearing of certain symbols as a requirement of a dream. It was sung at the Sun Dance during the time that the dancers were resting, everyone listening attentively. The song commences:

'anpe wi kin	the sun
kola waye lo	is my friend
cangle ska le	a hoop
koyag maye lo	it has made me wear
wanbli wan	an eagle
koyag maye lo'	it has made me wear

LAKOTA DREAM SONG[27]

Costume was a vital component of a dance. Californian tribes were expert in working with bird feathers, large or small. This Luiseño apron or cape – perhaps it could be described as a kilt – of golden eagle feathers (above) is attached to a netted band leaving the feathers free to rise and fall with the dancer's movements. It was used in an Eagle Dance.

One of the most common instruments alongside the drum was the rattle. This Kumeyaay example (left) consists of 22 polished deer toes which were shaken in order to produce a gentle percussive sound; perhaps the sort of sound best suited to solemn occasions.

A drummer beats out a rhythm to accompany a guessing game being played by these Winnebago Indians (right), music being an often-present feature of daily life.

This gourd rattle (below) was loaded with pebbles and was used by the lead singer or shaman during a Cherokee dance. The sound produced was often identified ceremonially and symbolically as rain, the renewer of land and life.

Musical Instruments

A widespread instrument was the flageolet, which although mainly used for courting was, on occasions in the Woodlands, employed to warn a village of an approaching war-party and in several Pueblo ceremonials, used to accompany songs. The flageolet, the precursor of the modern flute, was of ancient origin and was widely distributed in North America. Thus, Captain John Smith observed its use in the early-17th century among the Indians of Virginia. 'For their musicke they use a thicke cane, on which they pipe as on a recorder'.[28]

There were several variants of the early form of flute.[29] In the Woodlands, it was often made of two sections of cedar joined to form a cylinder some 18 in (46cm) long and an inch in diameter. A solid section was left near the top with an opening cut on each side over which was fitted a pitch control of wood. As Ritzenthaler reports 'The musician produced the tones by fingering six holes spaced about an inch apart. The flute was end-blown and was strictly a solo instrument'.[30] Some tribes insisted that the youths played the flutes **outside** the village as it was thought that soft, sweet and pleasant tones were just too seductive for unmarried girls to resist![31]

Of the musical instruments, however, it was the drum which figured most prominently, the steps of the dancers following its rhythm rather than that of the song. The drum beat governed the bodily movements while the song voiced the emotion of the appeal to the higher powers.

The shaman's drum of the North Alaskan Eskimo was larger than those used in social dances and singing, various tricks being performed with it, such as when drumming 'tobacco leaves appeared' on the rawhide head, while Haida shamans' drums were – together with a rattle and soul catcher – considered essential ele-

ments in the exorcism of sickness from a patient's body.[32]

More specialized was the water drum, particularly popular with the Chippewa for use in the *Midewiwin* ceremonials. It was considered a sacred instrument and never used without due respect. Made from a hollowed out basswood log, it was sealed at the bottom with pitch to make it water tight. A hole with a fitted plug was made in one side and a piece of heavy tanned buckskin was stretched over the top by means of a hoop. Water was introduced through the hole perhaps to a depth of three or four inches, the depth determining the amount of reverberation, while the tone was changed by more or less damping of the drum head by shaking.[33] When struck with a curved drum stick, the dampened head emitted a deep soft tone with great carrying power.

Dance

Dancing frequently accompanied musicians and singers, it being an important element of ceremonial and ritual. Some dances were peculiar to men and others to women; some dances belonged to specially elected individuals, such as the *Onthonrontha* 'one chants' of the Iroquois, while others were for all who wished to take part. Still others were for members of certain orders, societies or fraternities, such as the Chippewa Dream Dance which used a sacred drum and was almost a 'drum religion'. Thus, there were personal, fraternal, clan, tribal and intertribal dances with various components of social, comic, mimic, military, patriotic, invocative, mourning and erotic actions. Many were expressions of both thanksgiving and gratitude, such as the *Moki* (California) *Hesi* Society which celebrated all the seasonal events and honored the animal spirits or the Ute Bear Dance (Basin) honoring that animal in order to acquire its hunting and sexual prowess.[34]

The Buffalo Dance

Among the most spectacular were the buffalo-calling dances reported on by early observers of the Prairie and Plains tribes. The explorer, Maximilian, who traveled to the Plains tribes in 1832-34, describes such a dance for the Mandan:

> 'The eight buffalo bulls put on this fantastic dress in the lodge, . . . (they) march out two abreast in an inclined posture, extending their robes with outspread hands, and holding the willow fans upright . . . When they are opposite to each other they stand upright and imitate the roaring of the buffalo . . .'.[35]

Catlin (1833) refers to this as the *Bel-lohck nah-pick* or 'bull dance' and describes the accompanying music, 'all unite to them their voices, raised to the highest pitch possible, as the music for the bull-dance, which is then commenced and continued for fifteen minutes or more in perfect time, and without cessation or intermission.'[36]

The Dance Repertoires

Dance repertoires were extensive among most tribes. Thus, Lewis Henry Morgan in discussing Iroquois ceremonial, lists some 38 major dances of the Seneca, 11 of which were for men only, seven for women only, 14 for mixed groups and six where elaborate costume was worn.[37] Several of such dances – 'Our Life Supporter Dances' – honored the growth and gift of corn, beans and squash.[38] They were also performed as the principal rituals of the Green Corn ceremonies, performed in the Iroquois longhouses, 'the council house of the faithful'.[39] Such ceremonials could continue for three days or longer. The longhouse was rectangular with a fireplace (today a stove) located at or near each end. Seating was along the walls which left most of the floor space available for the dancing which was 'such an important part of the ritual'.[40]

Instruments were, of course, subject to regional variations. This Haida whistle from Skidegate (above) represents a mountain demon's call and is typical Northwest Coast in carving style. The less elaborate double whistle (below) is also from Skidegate.

was much favored by young vigorous dancers who, by elastic steps and using only the ball of the foot, knees lifted high, moved rapidly across the dance ground. Employed in several episodes of the spectacular Hoop Dance – a solo dance which probably originated in the Southwest – it was almost as common as the toe-heel with similar distribution and popularity. [42]

Games

As well as song and dance, games were an important component in the daily lives of the American Indian, often with much associated ceremonial and pageantry. The wide variety of games which were played throughout the nine cultural areas, can be broadly divided into two main classes – those of dexterity and those of chance. Games of dexterity were archery, javelin throwing in various forms, shooting at a moving target, ball games and racing. Games of chance were various styles of dice where different objects, marked or shaped a certain way, were thrown at random to obtain a score. Other games of chance were guessing games where one or more players had to guess in which two or more places a marked object was concealed.

Hidden-ball Game

In the Hopi version, which was played by women and referred to as *bakshiwu*, a ball is hidden under one of four carved and painted cottonwood cups, the object being to guess under which it is concealed. A variant of this was the Moccasin game, so called because a moccasin was used to conceal the ball. Played almost exclusively by men, it was particularly popular among the Algonquian tribes in the north, such as the Cree, Blackfeet and Chippewa, who in turn probably influenced the Siouan and Iroquoian tribes, since it is also found among them. [43] 'Moccasin' was played as a gambling game and always accompanied by singing and drumming, its origins almost certainly based on a modification of the Navajo 'hidden-ball' game. [44]

The flageolet was one of the popular flute-type instruments used by Native Americans, frequently being used in courting. This example (above left) was collected from the Pima. It is incised but the significance of the marks is not known.

This deer dewclaw rattle (above right) formed part of the regalia of the Crazy Dog Society dancers of the Hidatsa It can be seen in the portrait earlier (see page 41) where the dancer holds one in his right hand.

Dance Styles and Steps

While the motion of men in dance was often vigorous with changes of position rapid, sometimes even violent, that of the women tended to be less so, although some dances did involve a leap or hop, and alternately moving each shoulder slightly to give a distinctive swaying motion. Interestingly, among the Onondaga, Cayuga and other Iroquois tribes, one of the names for woman was *wathonwisas* 'she sways or rocks' which was a term taken from the swaying or rocking motion which women used in dancing. [41]

One of the widest distributed and most used dance steps was the toe-heel. On the **loud** beat of the drum, the toe of one foot lightly touches the ground, on the next **soft** beat the heel comes hard down on the ground; now the other foot is put forward, the action repeated alternating from one foot to the next. Performed slow or fast, these basic steps were used throughout the cultural areas – not only in the Buffalo Dances and Life Supporter Dances of the Plains and Woodlands but also in the hunting dances of the Pueblos and the famed Mountain Spirit Dance of the Apaches.

Another step was the hop-step. A type of skipping movement with a double hop on each foot, it

A group of men playing a hand game (left), an immensely popular form of gambling, often with very high stakes.

This set of gambling sticks in a leather pouch (below) was obtained from the Tlingit in 1882. Sticks of this kind were sometimes inlaid with abalone.
Among some Northwest Coast tribes winners of games of chance were esteemed for their skill and spiritual endowment, their good fortune considered as a gift from unseen powers.

The Hand Game

One of the commonest and undoubtedly the most widely distributed of guessing games, being found in various forms among 28 different linguistic groups and 81 tribes[45] was the Hand Game. Two or four bone or wooden cylinders, one plain and one marked, are held in the hands by one player, the other side guessing in which hand the unmarked cylinder is concealed; the game was commonly counted with sticks which were stuck in the ground between the players. Although there were considerable variations in the game, one marked advantage is that it can be played entirely by gesture so that the sign language was sufficient. It is probably for this reason that the game was so widely distributed.

Although children did not participate in the adult games, they were often observers and a description by the ethnologist, James Mooney, of an Arapaho game, gives a particularly good insight into the social atmosphere in which Indian children spent the long winter evenings:

'This is a favorite winter game with the prairie tribes . . . It is played by both men and women, but never by the two sexes together.

It is the regular game in the long winter nights after the scattered families have abandoned their exposed summer positions on the open prairie, and moved down near one another in the shelter of the timber along the streams. When hundreds of Indians are thus camped together, the sound of the drum, the rattle, and the gaming song resound nightly through the air . . .
The players sit in a circle around the *tipi* fire, those on one side of the fire playing against those on the other. The only requisites are the 'button' or *gaqaa*, usually a small bit of wood, around which is tied a piece of string or otter skin, with a pile of tally sticks . . . All this time the opposing players are watching the hands of the other, or looking straight into their faces to observe every telltale movement of their features, and when one

These four Zuni boys (right) are painted with their clan markings and prepared for a springtime kicking stick race. The runners balance the stick then throw them forward – perhaps as far as 100ft (30m) – and chase in pursuit in a race that might last 25 miles (40km). For identification, the sticks bear the markings of the particular clan.

These gaming arrows (below) are from the Kiowa. Made of a single piece of maple wood they have been intricately painted with designs that relate to aspects of their cosmology. The arrows are about 2$\frac{1}{2}$ft (76cm) long and were thrown like a javelin. The objective was to see who could throw them the furthest.

thinks he has discovered in which hand the button is, he throws out his thumb toward that hand with a loud "that" . . . So the play goes on until the small hours of the night. It is always a gambling game, and the stakes are sometimes very large'.[46]

Archery

Simple archery, that is shooting at a stationary mark, was widely practiced in various forms, and targets made of grass, bark and wood have been described for most regions. More skilled, however, was to hit a bundle tossed into the air before it hit the ground.[47] A favorite of the Mandan, according to Catlin, was 'the game of the arrow':

'The young men who are the most distinguished in this exercise, assemble on the prairie at a little distance from the village, and having paid, each one, his "entrance-fee", such as a shield, a robe, a pipe, or other article, step forward in turn, shooting their arrows into the air, endeavouring to see who can get the greatest number flying in the air at one time, thrown from the same bow'.[48]

Ball Games

Ball games were particularly popular, a definite feature of all of them being that the ball was seldom touched by hand, being strictly 'forbidden by the rules of the game'.[49]

North American ball games have been classified as 'racket', in which the ball is tossed with a racket of some sort; 'shinny', in which the ball is struck with a wooden club or bat; 'double ball', a game mainly confined to women and played with two balls tied together which are tossed with a stick; and a type of ball 'race' where a ball or round stick was kicked.

Strachey, who served as a Secretary of the Jamestown colony in the period 1611-13, referred to the local Indians as playing a game like 'a kynd of exercise they have often amongst them much like that which boyes call bandy (hockey) in England',[50] and the Powhatan Indians were described as fond of football 'only the foot could be used to move the ball toward the goal. It required a great deal of speed and dexterity on the part of the player'.[51]

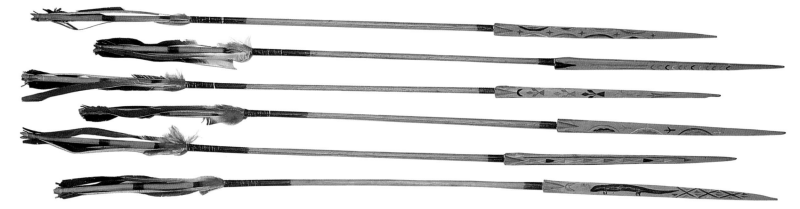

Ball games were of ancient origin and virtually a national pastime among the Southeastern tribes, such as the Choctaw, Cherokee and Creeks. That which resembled lacrosse and called by the Choctaw *ishtaboli*,[52] the excitement of which particularly caught the explorer, George Catlin's attention, was described by him in the summer of 1834:

'I have made it an uniform rule, whilst in the Indian country, to attend every ball-play I could hear of, if I could do it by riding a distance of twenty or thirty miles; and my usual custom has been on such occasions, to straddle the back of my horse, and look on to the best advantage. In this way I have sat, and oftentimes reclined, and almost dropped from my horse's back, with irresistible laughter at the succession of droll tricks, and kicks and scuffles which ensue, in the almost superhuman struggles for the ball. These plays generally commence at nine . . . in the morning (and) . . . from that time till near sundown, without more than one minute of intermission at a time, before the game has been decided'.[53]

Ball games utilizing various sticks were prevalent throughout North America. One of the most popular games was lacrosse, depicted here (below) by Seth Eastman being played among the Sioux. The Creek, Cherokee and Choctaw had played a version in the Southeast since ancient times, and among the Cherokee the 'companion of battle' was second only to war as a manly pursuit. In order to play one had to be ritually pure and sound of body and character. These trunks (below left) were worn in Cherokee games during the 1880s. The sticks (left) are made of split wood with bark wrappings and bent into a loop to form a ball-catching pocket usually made from hemp or twisted squirrel skin.

The ball games Catlin witnessed among the Choctaw were epic and small wonder the name was often translated as 'little brother of war'. One can imagine the spectacle of mayhem ensuing when 6-700 able-bodied young warriors armed with sticks compete with one another for the ball. Catlin wrote, 'In these struggles, every mode is used that can be devised, to oppose the progress of the foremost, who is likely to get the ball; and these obstructions often meet desperate individual resistance, which terminates in a violent scuffle'.(Letters and notes, vol.II,p.126.)

Two settlements or even tribes played against each other, the numbers varying between about 10 to up to hundreds on each side – the latter providing for a particularly dramatic spectacle!

Catlin captured the atmosphere of one game he witnessed near Fort Gibson in 1834, and recorded some important details of the arrangements. At sundown, we

'witnessed the ceremony of measuring out the ground, and erecting the "byes" or goals which were to guide the play. . . These goals were about forty or fifty rods apart; and at a point just half way between, was another small stake, driven down, where the ball was to be thrown up at the firing of a gun, to be struggled for by the players . . . This game had been arranged . . . three or four months before the parties met to play it, . . . soon after dark, a procession of lighted flambeaux was seen coming from each encampment, to the ground where the players assembled around their respective byes; and at the beat of the drums and chaunts of the women, each party of players commenced the "ball-play dance" '.[54]

Catlin continues and describes the player's costume: 'a breech-cloth around his waist, with a beautiful bead belt, and a "tail", made of white horsehair or quills, and a "mane" on the neck, of horsehair dyed of various colours'.[55] No moccasins were worn. The game commenced the following morning the ball being thrown at the firing of a gun

'when an instant struggle ensued between the players, who were some six or seven hundred in numbers, . . . running together and leaping, actually over each other's heads, and darting between their adversaries' legs. . . and every voice raised to the highest key . . . there are rapid successions of feats, and of incidents, that astonish and amuse far beyond the conception of any one who has not had the singular good luck to witness them'.[56]

A number was agreed on for the maximum score and the party who first gets this number wins; in the case of the game witnessed by Catlin, it was 100.

Stakes were sometimes more than mere 'goods and chattels' as reported by Catlin. Thus, one ball game reported on between the Creeks and Choctaws which took place about 1790, was actually for the possession of a beaver pond on the Noxubee River. Unfortunately, although on the face of it the ball game was replacing the moral equivalent of war, some of the competitions ended in a battle![57]

The Hoop and Pole Game

Another widely distributed athletic game – played in various forms throughout North America – was the 'Hoop and Pole', where a netted hoop, somewhat resembling a spider's web, was rolled along the ground and then thrown at with arrows or spears, the count being deter-

Hopi boys played a throwing game in their mesa villages which consisted of a cornhusk ring and corncob darts (above). The darts were flighted with feathers and fitted with a sharp point. The game could be played at any time but it was thought to be most beneficial to do so when the ceremonial season came to a close after the harvests.

Hoop and pole was a simple and popular game in many regions. This picture (left) shows San Carlos Apache men at play with their slender sticks of willow. Their hoop is made of bent wood lashed with sinew.

mined by the point at which the missile strikes the hoop. The game, according to Culin, was exclusive to males and the number of players varied from two upward.[58] The anthropologist George Bird Grinnell, reported for the Montana Blackfeet, that it was a favorite pastime in the day, the hoop used by that tribe being almost 4in (10cm) in diameter.

> 'A level, smooth piece of ground was selected, at each end of which was placed a log. At each end of the course were two men, who gambled against each other. A crowd always surrounded them, betting on the sides. The wheel was rolled along the course, and each man at the end whence it started, darted an arrow at it. The cast was made just before the wheel reached the log at the opposite end of the track.' Grinnell concluded that 'it was a very difficult game, and one had to be very skillful to win'.[59]

Not so popular as the Ball Game but obviously of considerable antiquity, was the *Chunkey* of the Creek, Cherokee and other tribes in the Southeast. In place of the wooden or cedar ring, a stone disk was used.[60]

Given its popularity in many regions, it was to be expected that many varieties of hoop and pole existed. The Chiricahua Apache might use twig and sinew (above right), while this small yucca hoop and incised spear (right) belonged to the Zuni clowns known as *koyemshi* or Mud Heads.

An ancient game of many variants existed in the Southeast called Chunky in which a shaped stone (right) was hurled with great force along a cleared alley while two players threw lances at it.

Another variant of the basic Hoop and Pole game was developed for playing in a confined space by the Central Eskimo of the Cumberland Sound region and was referred to as *nuglutang*. Here, a small rhomboidal of ivory with a hole in the center was hung from the ceiling of the igloo, it being steadied by a piece of ivory or a heavy stone hanging from its lower end. The players stood around the suspended plate, and at a signal from the winner of the previous game, everyone attempted to thread the hole with a thin pointed stick, the one who succeeded being the winner. The distinguished anthropologist Franz Boas, who reported on this game and who had witnessed it firsthand, recorded that the 'game is always played amid great excitement'.[61]

The Ceremonial of Games

While it was widely recognized that many of the games played a key role in the development of qualities and skills necessary for survival – the coordination of mind and muscle, the development of keen ears and eyes, strength, stability, stamina, bravery and confidence – another important aspect was the associated religious connotation. Such activities were associated with the curing of sickness, to initiate fertilization and to insure the continued reproduction of animals and plants and, particularly in the arid regions of the Southwest, to bring rain.[62]

The games often reveal the nature of the habitat, habits and major occupations of those who played them. As one authority on the subject observed, 'It is not surprising that hunting was featured in a number of games of the Plains and

Woodland tribes; corn, weather, and grain in those of the Southwest; and fishing, salmon, and seal in the games of the fishermen of the Northwest Coast.'[63]

References to games also occur in many of the myths of the tribes, particularly those relating to the origin of the world, animals and mankind. Generally, they are in the form of some type of contest in which a culture hero overcomes his opponents. These culture heroes were viewed as the original patrons of the games which were ultimately played by mankind.[64]

Certain seasons or times were often observed for the playing of several games, determined by such factors as success in the hunting or drying of salmon and the planting and harvesting of corn, or they were related to the signs of natural phenomena, such as the phases of the moon or the seasons of the winds. Thus, the Makah of the Northwest Coast played a form of shinny after they had caught and killed a whale.[65]

The power of the winds was alluded to in the Omaha's ball game of *tabe gaci*, played between two divisions of the tribe and said to have a cosmic significance where the 'initial movements of the ball referred to the winds, the bringers of life'.[66]

Many of the objects used in the various games, be they of chance or dexterity, were among some of the most significant artifacts placed upon the religious altars, such as those associated with the Zuni and Hopi War Gods and the Arapaho Sun Dance.[67] The same objects were also attached to various forms of ceremonial regalia, such as headdresses and masks;[68] this is in addition to the special costume sometimes associated with a particular game as exemplified by that of Catlin's Choctaw ball player.[69]

Music, song, dance and games were thus vital components in the daily life and activities of the people, and essential factors in the yearly cycle of social and ceremonial organization.

Many games were accompanied by significant ceremonies. Catlin painted a scene called Ball-play Dance (left) where the game was started and judged by four respected shamans. They can be seen here at the center smoking to the Great Spirit seeking success in judging rightly and impartially in the important affair. While the menfolk work themselves up at either end, the women can be seen formed into two rows between the men, dancing and singing and imploring the Great Spirit to favor their side – on which they had waged valuable goods.

THE HOME AND DOMESTIC LIFE

When the Spanish first made contact with the Timucuan tribes of Northern Florida in the early-16th century,[2] they described the use of compactly built and stockaded towns, the houses being circular structures of poles and thatched with palmetto leaves. At the center was a large square in which stood the townhouse for tribal gatherings. Later, these Timucuan and other tribes farther west, such as the Algonquian groups in present-day North Carolina, were visited by the artists Jacques le Moyne de Morgues in 1564 and John White, who was on Sir Walter Raleigh's expedition, some 20 years later. Both men, with great attention to detail, recorded in paintings and copious notes, many aspects of Indian life in this New World and observed that some of their achievements, such as boat-making, weaponry, horticultural expertise, even the extraction of silver and gold from the streams, matched those of the seemingly more cultured Europeans. While dwellings varied somewhat (for example, the Algonquians utilized rectangular houses covered with reed mats and bark), most of the villages were securely stockaded with well-kept gardens in which were grown corn, pumpkins and tobacco. Surplus produce was carefully stored and preserved, particularly by the Timucuan groups and all used well-made clay pots in which stews were cooked.

Sadly, these early contacts – first with the Spaniards, later with the English and French – led to a progressive breakdown in tribal organization and decrease in population as the European colonization took effect with pillaging, enslavement, genocide and disease. By the early 1700s, very little was left of these impressive cultures; even the Calusas of southern Florida, who so fiercely held out against the Spanish, were forced to retreat to Havana.

These records, giving much detail of the early lifestyles in North America, tell us that a great deal which was observed later as explorers moved west – the fortified villages, central square with its meeting house, nearby cultivated fields and maximum use of the resources of the environment – was the product of an anciently established pattern, the basics of which were replicated throughout Woodlands, Prairies and Plains.

American Indian habitations, the product of an eon of experience, were designed and developed to keep rain, wind, heat and cold at bay, while village layout took into account defense and the religious and social requirements of the tribe. Needs varied from the hostile environment of the Arctic and Subarctic to the dry sweltering heat of the Southwest, from the damp and fog of the Northwest Coast to the bracing climate of the Atlantic seaboard, from the mild but humid Southeast to the sudden changes of the windswept Great Plains. With immense ingenuity in the use of local natural materials, emerged – to name but a few – the *igloo, wigwam, hogan, kiva,* plank house, longhouse, grasshouse, *chickee* and *tipi.*

A woman's skill at a craft very often provided her with status within her society. This was true of basketry in California and parts of the Northwest Coast – witness this beautiful Tlingit twined basket with naturally dyed grass design motifs (above left) – and of beadwork in the Plateau; this brightly colored beaded bag (right and far left) is Nez Perce. On the Plains a woman's skill in hide working was highly esteemed. The products of her labor – dependent on her husband's success in hunting – brought wealth and status to the family. Working a hide (main picture) was an arduous task. A *tipi* required a dozen or so hides and each hide took several days work. The fat and flesh was removed, then it was sun-dried, scraped and thinned. That was enough work for a robe or blanket, but hides for other purposes had to have the hair removed, then be tanned, stretched and softened.

These men were photographed building this snow house or *igloo* circa 1915 (right). Such houses were used from about October to May. It took geat skill and a knowledge of snow to complete the work. The people are probably Copper Inuit who used a distinctive flat-topped entrance to the *igloo* which is partly visible here. Once built, the women prepared the interior.

Habitations of the Eskimo

The term *igloo* was derived from an Eastern Eskimo dialect, *igdlu*, and was a habitation of ice and snow which was of a compression shell construction, the snow blocks serving as structural support and wall covering.[3] Although popularly associated with the Eskimo, the *igloo* was limited to the Central Arctic Eskimo, and far more common for winter use throughout this vast region of the Arctic, was the *karmak*, a partially subterranean earth-covered dwelling, while in the spring and through the summer, the *tupik*, a portable tent made of caribou or seal skins was used.[4]

Two skilled *igloo* builders could complete the basic hemisphere within a few hours, the type of snow being carefully selected; if too compacted, it would be almost impossible to cut with the antler or bone (later metal) knife and if too soft, the blocks would disintegrate under the compression. The snow blocks were built up in a spiral, progressively leaning inward until the whole house was closed in. Then, while the men were completing the tunnel-like entrance, the slits and holes in the main dome were filled in by the less skilled women and children, who also covered the exterior with snow using wooden shovels. A piece of clear ice was set into the wall just above the entrance which gave light in the house and a small air hole was bored in the roof nearby, which could be covered with a piece of hide. Once a small lamp was lit within the *igloo*, the surface snow melted and then almost immediately refroze so that the inner surface became coated with a thin layer of ice. A firm platform ran all the way around the interior of the *igloo*, covered with sticks, mats and tanned caribou skins; this was used for sitting and sleeping. An average size *igloo* could shelter up to six people. However, since there was often much food and equipment to store, and possibly other relatives such as a young married couple to accommodate, the main habitation was not infrequently added to, so forming a cluster of interconnected – but generally smaller – *igloos*.

Similar in shape but of different construction was the *karmak*.[5] Here, a circular pit of required size was dug some five or six feet deep (1-2m), over which a dome-shaped frame of wood or whalebone was constructed. This was then unearthed and turfed over, the entrance being gained by an underground passageway.

In constructing their habitations, special taboos were frequently observed which suggests some symbolic association between the house and womb. Thus, 'special attention was given to the final building step: the opening for the keystone block had to be as large as possible to ensure easy childbirth for the women. If a family hoped for a son, that block had to be bigger than the block preceding it, and its softest side had to face the rear of the house'.[6]

Life Within an Arctic Dwelling

All explorers and observers of Eskimo life were immensely impressed by their ability to survive in the hostile Arctic environment, where temperatures could drop as low as 50 degrees below zero and the sun was blotted out for weeks, if not months, on end. Crucial to their survival, of course, were the *igloo* and *karmak* which, to the Eskimo, became their world and haven for the long and harsh winter period. This tiny space was a 'labyrinth alive with the movements of crowded people. No flat static walls arrest the ear or eye, but voices and laughter came from several directions and the eye can glance through here, past there, catching glimpses of the activities of nearly everyone'.[7]

It is little wonder, therefore, that the habitation itself reflected the divisions which were recognized in the external world. Thus, the excavated floor area, called the *Natiq*, was associated with men, their accoutrements and the sea in which they hunted. The raised sitting and sleeping platforms, referred to as *Ikliq*, were associated with women, the stone oil lamps which were in their care, and the land.[8]

The lamp was crucial to the sustaining of life within an Eskimo dwelling; cut from a soft soapstone and fueled by blubber or seal oil with a wick of long burning moss, it provided light and heat for both cooking and drying clothing.[9] Its effective

This semi-subterranean dwelling (above right) is typical of the varieties which existed in the region. A pit was covered with a log framework and then blanketed with earth or turf (occasionally stone and skins) to conserve heat. A central fire kept it warm, a hole in the roof provided ventilation and windows of translucent seal intestine might be instaled to let in light.

In the spring and summer a tent was used known as a *tupik*. This was made of animal skins strung on poles and anchored by rocks to counter the Arctic wind. This family (left) was pictured outside its *tupik*.

The Arctic was little different from most indigenous societies in North America in that the men hunted and maintained a readiness for war, while the women kept the home, made the clothing and prepared food. The Arctic woman had a hard life; scraping, cutting, drying, cleaning and manufacturing from (right) all the animal skins brought home was demanding enough on its own; in addition, in some Arctic communities it was taboo to assist a woman in childbirth and she was expected to manage this on her own.

operation, however, required considerable skill and the Eskimo woman needed to know this art to perfection, for there were few household possessions that played as big a part in their domestic life as the lamp. The wife tended to it and it was strictly under her jurisdiction:

> 'The more lamps she can take care of the cleverer she is, and many lamps are a sign of wealth and prestige . . . in a Polar Eskimo house, though, there were rarely more than two lamps, one on each side bunk. It is the younger woman who runs the household and has all the power. The widowed mother-in-law is a dethroned ruler. She loses her say over the lamps when her son brings home a wife, although the young bride may have a kind disposition and leave her one lamp to take care of. In these situations there are no false sentiments'.[10]

The soapstone lamp was kept burning at all times, and when the household prepared to sleep, the moss was adjusted to give a narrow flame and the reservoir filled with fresh oil or blubber.

> 'If it is properly regulated it burns easily through the period of sleep . . . by placing the lamp on three stones or on a tripod, and slanting it at the right angle, one can regulate the flow of blubber to the side where the moss-wick is [and] a stick serves to open or close the wick, making it narrow or wide according to whether a large or a small flame is wanted'.[11]

The lamp also served another important function – when the flame started to burn low, the flow of air through the dwelling was increased by changing the size of the air hole by readjusting the whisk of hay stuck in it.

Meat was traditionally cooked in pots of carved soapstone, removed with two pronged forks made of whalebone and eaten out of wooden plates. Ladles for soup, water and oil were carved from

musk-ox horns and eating spoons were made from caribou antlers. One most important and traditional tool used for cutting meat, skinning and making clothing, was the *ulu* which had a crescent-shaped blade with a wooden or bone handle. Favorite foods were thick blood soups and fresh caribou meat, supplemented by seal, walrus, whale, musk-ox and various kinds of fish depending upon the region.

An Eskimo lamp (right) was a small oval of hollowed-out soapstone with a wick of moss or heather. In a well-made *igloo* a single lamp could heat all its occupants and a temperature of 90 degrees fahrenheit could be maintained using blubber oil.

This interior view (left) shows how spacious an *igloo* could be for a family. Note the raised platform or *Ikliq* used by the women and children who are dressed in wterproof skin clothing, hair side inward for warmth and insulation.

The interiors of these dwellings were generally quite warm and dry and on entering the house, outer clothing and boots were removed, both men and women generally moving about in the house barefoot and wearing only their trousers.[12]

Women spent a good deal of their time making and repairing clothing:

'Like a Turkish tailor, she sits with her legs stretched out at right angles to the body, her favorite position, with her work between her toes . . . from intuition, she cuts her skins in the proper pieces and sews them together, rarely measuring anything. . . with small, hardly visible stitches she weaves her narwhal sinew thread in and out until the skin pieces look as if they had grown together'.[13]

Men made and repaired their hunting equipment, carved the horn and soapstone utensils and made ivory and bone adornments, such as labrets, buttons and pendants.

Many settlements consisted of several dwellings, generally occupied by related families and not infrequently linked together by a complex of tunnels. A central meeting place was the men's *Kashim* and here boys listened and watched the men, progressively identifying with them, thus learning their crafts, mythology and lore. Similarly, girls associated with the women to learn the essentials for survival – skinning of animals, production of waterproof clothing and the handling of the essential soapstone lamp.

Such experience gave rise to a traditional Eskimo personality as exemplified by that of the Alaskan Eskimo which has been described as a 'Spartan ethic'.[14] According to this standard, an individual was expected to develop and display the qualities of competence, discipline and toughness, both physical and mental, in virtually all spheres of activity and such characteristics

The *ulu* was the utilitarian tool par excellence. Metal bladed with a wooden or bone handle, it was used for a myriad of tasks from cutting and scraping skins to the preparation of food.

59

'were presented to others through quality performance, a dignified bearing, and emotional restraint'.[15]

The Longhouse of the Iroquois

In contrast to the Eskimo's use of snow, ice and earth to construct their dwellings, the tribes of the Northeastern Woodlands utilized a material which abounded in their domain – bark. One of the most impressive bark structures was the Iroquois *Ho-de'-no-sote*, or 'Longhouse' from which they called themselves, 'as one confederated people, *Ho-de'-no-sau-nee* (People of the Long-House)'.[16] Described as 'a most conspicuous feature of the Iroquois settlements'[17], it consisted of a strong frame of upright poles set in the ground, which were stabilized with horizontal poles and surmounted by a round, later triangular, roof. The frame was covered with large pieces of elm bark stripped from the tree during early summer when the sap was rising. The dampened sheets some 6ft (2m) long and just over a foot (30cm) wide, were first flattened under heavy rocks and then attached to the longhouse frame. One early (circa 1715) observer described the

sheets as lapping 'one over the other like slate' and that they were 'secured outside with fresh poles similar to those which form the frame roof underneath, and are still further strengthened by long pieces of saplings split in two, and are fastened to the extremities of the roof, on the sides, or on the wings, by pieces of wood cut with hooked ends, which are regularly spaced for this purpose'.[18]

The houses were, on average, 25ft (7.6m) or so wide, the length depending upon the number of families to be sheltered and while 80ft (24m) was the average, houses of up to 200ft (61m) in length were commonly used by the Mohawk. The dwelling was divided into a series of compartments running each side of the house; these were closed on three sides but open toward a central aisle where there was a small fire which was shared by two directly opposite families of some five to six individuals. Raised bunks covered with reed mats and tanned deerskins, ran along the three walls and these served as seats during the day and beds at night. Above the bunks were long shelves on which food and clothing could be stacked and between each compartment were

This bark-covered dwelling (right) is a type of longhouse, although not as high as many of the more typical Iroquoian kind each of which accommodated up to 20 related families. Light and air entered the dwelling via the door at each end and through smoke holes centered above the hearth in each family compartment. In ventilation terms this provision was often minimal and the atmosphere within a longhouse could become sooty and stale.

bark bins which were used to store dried maize, fruit and meat, while suspended by cords from the roof-poles were further supplies of corn, braided by the husks, together with dried squashes and pumpkins. The 'apartments' were described as 'warm, roomy, and tidily-kept habitations'.[19]

They were, however, much more than this for, after the foundation of the League of the Iroquois in the 15th century and for some 200 years, the longhouse was seen as the unifying political symbol of the five tribes – Mohawk, Oneida, Onondaga, Cayuga and Seneca – who spoke metaphorically of their domain, as a gigantic Longhouse, which stretched 240 miles (386km) from near Albany to the shores of Lake Erie at Buffalo. As the scholar, Lewis Henry Morgan, observed 'the League was not like a Longhouse. It *was* a Longhouse, extending from the Hudson to the Genesee, in which around five fires the five tribes gathered'.[20]

The longhouse was not exclusive to the Iroquois but was used also by the Huron who lived to the north on the eastern shores of present-day Lake Huron. Here, however, in a region traditionally described as 'Huronia', the difference in the resources of the two environments dictated the use of cedar rather than elm bark. Nevertheless, living styles were markedly similar and for the Huron, as for the Iroquois, the longhouse reflected much of the physical manifestation of their economic and social system. It was in these surroundings that the key elements of economic cooperation, family solidarity and rule by mutual agreement, found their fundamental expression and, in turn, these values 'were projected to the village through kinship ties and ultimately to the tribal level'.[21]

The *Wigwam*

A much smaller dwelling than the Iroquois Longhouse but which invariably utilized a bark and mat covering, was the *wigwam*, an Abnaki (Algonquian) name, literally meaning 'dwelling'. Several other house-types were used by the

Woodland Indians – the peaked lodge (which resembled the *tipi* in appearance) and the bark house. However, the dome-shaped structure so characteristic of the *wigwam* was widely distributed from Canada to North Carolina.

The Chippewa *Wigwam*

Among the best documented is the Chippewa *wigwam* which they called *waginogan*,[22] the materials for fabrication being saplings, bullrushes and birch bark tied together with basswood twine or bark strips. Although the *wigwam* could be oval or round and of variable size, its main characteristic was a dome-shaped top and its style of framing 'exemplified [the features of] tensile construction'.[23] The building of the Chippewa *wigwam* was a joint effort, the men cutting the saplings which were used for the frame, the women weaving the bullrush and bark coverings

A traditional Algonquian *wigwam* (above) photographed in 1873, conical in shape and with a frame of poles lined with bark and grass matting. The covering material was easy to transport and reuse, the materials readily available in the heavily wooded Northeast. This example is Micmac, one of the eastern Algonquian groups of the coastal zone. The woman wears a mixture of traditional and Euroamerican clothing.

This bark-covered lodge (above) of the Minnesota Ojibwa was photographed circa 1890. The lodge contains elements of the other two: the longhouse-shape with the matting exterior combined with the exterior poles which were used to hold the bark sheets in place.

leaving or entering. The cooking was generally done by the mother of the family who, after preparation of the food, passed portions to the various family members. Special attention was given to the requirements of the young men – the hunters and protectors – and a large piece of meat would be sent to them, each cutting off what he required.

Traditionally, each branch of the family was allocated a position within the *wigwam*: opposite the entrance and beyond the central fire was the honored position for grandparents; either side of the entrance were the parents, while daughters and sons were between mother and grandmother, father and grandfather.

The floor of the *wigwam* was generally covered with small cedar branches on top of which was laid rush matting. Rolled up mats around the sides of the *wigwam* served as seats during the day, then, at night, were unrolled for use as bedding, being covered with a thin mattress made of hide or cloth filled with feathers. As one observer reported, the interior of the wigwam was a warm and snug winter abode and

'The winter evenings were social and pleasant. The fire burned brightly, but no work was done which placed a strain on the eyes. A favorite pastime was the making of birch bark transparencies. The woman made basswood cord or fish nets and sometimes they made birch bark makuks or dishes. The young men reclined in the wigwam and always had a drum conveniently near them. Sometimes they went to call on the neighbors or to hear the story-tellers . . . The winter was the time for story-telling, and many old women were experts in this art'.[24]

The *Chickee*

In contrast to the *wigwam* of the Northeastern Woodlands, was the open-sided *chickee* of the Seminole and Miccosukee tribes who occupied the subtropical swamplands of Florida.[25] Made of cypress poles and either circular or rectangular in

and putting them into place. When the framework was complete, it was covered with overlapping bullrush mats which were tied to the frame. The top of the lodge was now covered with birch bark, first one layer across the shorter diameter and then another on top along the longer diameter leaving a gap for a smoke hole.

It was common to leave the *wigwam* frames standing when the group moved on; only the lightweight and carefully rolled up mats and sheets of birch bark were transported. Because of its easy transportation, the *wigwam* remained an extremely popular dwelling for centuries.

Living in the *Wigwam*

It was during the cold and long winter months, when all the family were at home, that the importance of the *wigwam* became particularly apparent in the life of the Woodland Indian.

Some *wigwams* were of sufficient length to allow the two or three generations who lived in it to have a separate fire at each end, a smoke hole over each. One unfailing rule, however, was that for protection the youngest individuals lived in the middle of the *wigwam*, passing their elders on

shape, it was thatched with palmetto fronds and generally partially walled, although in extreme hot and humid regions, these were absent. Most of the *chickees* had a raised floor area, either freestanding or attached to the upright cypress posts which was used as a working space during the day and for beds at night. Ventilation was both above and below these platforms which also protected the inhabitants from the swampland snakes, insects, alligators or sudden flooding.

A typical Seminole camp consisted of some four or five *chickees* to accommodate both families and guests and these were clustered around a communal cookhouse generally on islands – referred to as 'hammocks' – in the swamps and which could only be reached by means of a dugout canoe.

Central to the survival of the family was the large mortar and pestle which was fashioned from cypress logs and used for pounding corn for the drink, *sofkee*[26] or for mixing with dried meat.

The *chickee* design was ideal for the humid and hot climate of the swamplands, generally giving a good view of the rest of the camp and surrounding area and there was usually a breeze at the raised platform sleeping level due to the different tem-

A Mikasuki Seminole settlement (above) on a small island or hammock in the Big Cypress Swamp, Florida, in 1910. It shows the dugout canoe dock in the foreground and the open-ended cookhouse structure in the center rear. The *chickees* at either side were well designed for this semitropical climate. Canopies could be lowered from the roof at night to protect against mosquitoes and dew.

Corn has long been regarded in the Southeast as a life-sustaining gift of the gods and for centuries women have ground the kernels in hollowed-out tree trunk mortars (left) in order to create staples such as corn broth and sour corn bread.

Introduced by the Spanish, together with the horse, sheep have long been indispensable to the Navajo and this woman (below) is watching protectively over her precious flock. Among the Navajo a man's wealth was counted in horses, a woman's in sheep. The Navajo learned to move their flocks to fresh pasture but instead of using a lone shepherd, as was the European practice, the entire family uprooted and moved three or more times a year. The sheep, of course, provided the wool from which distinctive high quality blankets and rugs were woven.

peratures inside and out. The dwelling too matched the sudden and violent changes in weather conditions and hurricanes – which could flatten brick buildings – hardly affected the sturdy, pliant *chickee*.[27]

Food

In general, far more meat was consumed in the northern regions than in the southern areas of the North American continent, the reverse being true for vegetal food. The Eskimo, Chipewayan and Montagnais groups of the Arctic and Subarctic almost exclusively existed on birds, fish, seal, whale, caribou, musk-ox and even porcupines, and while occasionally supplemented with wild berries, nuts and green shoots, these were used more as seasonings.[28] In marked contrast – in addition to the extensive use of maize (discussed later in this chapter) – tribes of the Southwest such as the Hopi, Zuni, Cochiti, Acoma and Oraibi of New Mexico and Arizona grew beans, potatoes, peas, pumpkins, squashes, melons and chili. Wild plants were also very impor-

tant in the Southwestern diet, various seeds, roots, grasses and leaves of young plants being seasonally harvested and stored; if crops failed, the increased use of these valuable natural resources, prevented starvation. Meat was relatively unimportant although deer, birds and some buffalo meat from the Plains region supplemented the diet. Fish, so important in the north and on the Plateau, was generally avoided, the Navajo and Apache, for example, having a taboo against eating this creature.

Drinks

Water was the most common drink of the Indians and to ensure that there was always enough for their daily use villages were generally near to lakes, rivers and streams. Tea-like beverages were produced from various infusions of plants and plant parts. A drink made from manzanita berries was popular with the Californian tribes and one made from cactus fruit was favored by the Pima and adjacent tribes in Arizona. The Indians from the Woodlands used a root of the sassafras tree; dried and cut into small pieces, it was boiled to make a pleasant tasting tea. The leaves of such plants as Labrador tea, wintergreen, root bark of the raspberry, small twigs of the sweet birch and chokecherry bark were other sources for tea-like drinks. Several were drunk as medicines; the Blackfeet and other northern Plains tribes used yarrow boiled in water as a general purgative and as a cure for stomach and headache afflictions and the famous 'Black drink' (Carolina tea) made by boiling leaves of *Ilex cassine* in water was employed in the Southeast for ceremonial purification.[29] In the Historic Period, coffee and tea were traded to most tribes when sometimes they were compacted into soap-like bars for easy transport, thin portions being shaved off when needed.

Rice

Wild plants were an important component in the diet of most tribes who lived south of the Subarctic region, the abundance of a particular

species being determined by prevailing environmental factors. In the eastern Woodlands, a land of lakes, rivers and streams, the Chippewa harvested the vast stretches of wild rice which grew along the shores of lakes and rivers in much of present-day Minnesota, Michigan, Wisconsin and southern Canada. It was gathered just before it ripened, from canoes poled out to the wild rice beds. The stalks were bent over into the canoe and the heads of the plants struck with a flat tool so that the grains fell into the bottom of the boat. The rice was first dried in the sun, then beaten to loosen the hulls and finally, winnowed in large birch bark trays separating hulls from grain. After washing, it was ready either for cooking or to be stored away for future use.

Root Vegetables

Camas (*Camassia asculenta*) was a most important wild vegetable to many of the Plateau tribes such as the Nez Perce, Cayuse, Walla-Walla and Shoshoni. The liliaceous, onion-shaped bulb, was gathered in enormous quantities in the wet upland meadows which were a feature of much of the Plateau region. Gathered in early summer and again in the fall, they were dug out of the ground with a digging stick with a fire-hardened point and having a bone or wood cross-piece at the top. While gathered entirely by women, the expeditions to the camas meadows were generally viewed as a 'vacation' away from the home grounds and it was a time when children could swim in the nearby streams and rivers, while the men could fish and hunt. Agreeable to taste and highly nutritious, camas could be eaten raw but was generally cooked in an earth oven and made into sun-dried loaves for future use.[30] Other plants used by the Plateau tribes were kouse, which had a tuberous-like root and bitterroot (*Lewisia rediviva* Pursh). It is said that this latter root contained 'so much concentrated nutriment that a single ounce in the dried state is sufficient for a meal'.[31] These dried roots were an important component in the Plateau Indian diet; additionally, packed in the famous cornhusk bags, they

As shown by the items here (left) household pieces made by Indians could be simple and utilitarian, and not necessarily always aesthetically pleasing. All three Hidatsa pieces (top) are pottery water jars used for cooking. They are made from clay tempered with crushed rock, shaped by a paddle and anvil technique and then fired. The center one has a stand made of willow twigs and bark. The Apache preferred working with basketry, even for waterproof containers – an exception among the items here (below left) is the incised gourd dipper (top). The Apache made their basketry leakproof by sealing it with melted piñon pitch – an ingenious method since if a pot began to leak the pitch could just be reheated and smoothed over the hole. The twined jar (bottom) has been waterproofed with piñon pitch and would have been carried suspended from the tumpline across the top of the head. It could carry water or *tiswin*, a corn beer drunk by men. The basket (center) is clay-coated and is of the type used to cook corn in.

The Hopi grew a variety of fruit and vegetables – apricots, beans, squash – as well as more than two dozen varieties of corn. The corn was usually left in kernels for storage, then worked as required. The fruit and vegetables were sun-dried so that they could be stored through the winter months. Here (right) a Hopi girl sits surrounded by drying peppers or chilis and holding a typical sifter tray made of split yucca leaves.

This early coiled Apache basket (below) was used to prepare and serve food. The knife was used to trim the leaves off mescal tubers which were used as a foodstuff.

were used in trade to both the tribes of the Northwest Coast and the Plains Indians to the east.

The Piñon Complex

There was a similar system for the region of the Great Basin-land for such tribes as the Ute, Paiute, Bannock and Shoshoni. Here several very specific subsistence technologies for utilization of the flora and fauna of the region led to a foraging-type economy unmatched in the other cultural areas. Various seeds, roots, corms, berries, acorns, mesquite beans and stems

often required more or less complicated processing to make them edible. In particular, the gathering and processing of the seeds of nut pines – single and double-needled, sugar, limber and ponderosa – which began in late summer, was a major activity particularly of those groups who lived in the central core of the Great Basin. This so-called 'Piñon complex', involved not only gathering, processing and caching for winter use but also associated ceremonials of dancing and special prayers of thanksgiving were offered over the first seeds collected.[32]

The Pomme de Prairie

Although the Plains tribes placed great dependence on buffalo meat, they like all people subsisting on such an exclusive diet, had a great craving for vegetable foods. This was partially satisfied by harvesting the wild plant *Psoralea esculenta*, variously known as 'Indian bread root', 'Prairie turnip' or 'Pomme de Prairie' which was one of the most widely distributed wild food plants in the Great Plains area and which, prior to white agriculture, was found from Alberta and

Manitoba south-ward to Texas and New Mexico.[33] The elliptical tuber – about the size of a hen's egg – was a favorite food of not only Indians but also of the Plains grizzly bear. The tuber was usually found some 4-6in (10-15cm) below the surface of the ground. The crop was harvested using a digging stick from late spring through to midsummer. Its importance to the Plains Indian was reported on by the American explorer, William Clark, in May 1805:

'This root forms a considerable article of food with the Indians of the Missouri, who for this purpose prepare them in several ways. They are . . . gathered by the provident part of the natives for their winter store . . . [and] when well dried they will keep for several years . . . they usually pound them between two stones . . . untill (sic) they reduce it to a fine powder, thus prepared they thicken their soope (sic) with it'.[34]

Cultivated Plants

Tribes of the Southwest, Prairie (Eastern Plains) and Woodlands, cultivated various kinds of beans, squashes and pumpkins which although eaten fresh, were usually dehydrated and stored for future use. A major food plant in these cultural areas, however, was the giant cereal, maize, often referred to as 'Indian corn' or simply 'corn'.

It is probable that maize was introduced from Mexico long before the appearance of Europeans in North America; certainly, it may be inferred that it was extensively cultivated in prehistoric times when we consider the reports of some of the earliest explorers of the New World.[35] Thomas Hariot,[36] for example, who visited Virginia in 1586 and founded a plantation there, refers to the maize planting methods used by the local Indians, the seeds being sown in a small mound and carefully placed so as not to touch. Among the Iroquois, maize – together with beans and squash – was regarded as the most ancient of native food

staples and all three were considered as 'gifts from the Creator'.[37] This tribe, in common with many others, had elaborate ceremonials and the time of planting, ripening and harvesting, was generally the occasion for festivities.

Although the nomadic Plains tribes did not cultivate maize, the limited wild vegetables in their diet, led to a particular liking for garden produce.[38] In order to satisfy this need, southern Plains tribes – Kiowa, Comanche, Plains Apache – commonly traveled to the pueblos (Taos in New Mexico was a particularly popular rendezvous point) to trade for both fresh and dried corn, as well as beans, squash and pumpkins, while the more northern tribes – Cheyenne, Crow, Sioux and Assiniboin – exchanged their goods made from the products of the chase, such as pemmican, buckskin clothing, and *tipis* for the horticultural products produced by the Mandan, Hidatsa and Arikara village tribes on the Missouri River.

Maize and the Hidatsa Indians

The yearly cycle associated with maize is well-illustrated by that of the Hidatsa Indians, who lived in earth lodge villages on the banks of the Missouri in what is now present-day North Dakota.[39] Here, the low-lying well-watered lands, often located along the borders of streams, were designated as areas for growing maize, such plots varying from a small garden-like patch to up to three acres in extent. In early May, just as the snow was beginning to melt and while still occupying the winter village, the women's Goose Society began the year's agricultural activities and welcomed the corn spirits back from the south with ceremonies and dance.[40]

The Hidatsa cultivated the rich alluvial soil along the Missouri. The earth was worked by the women using hoes made from buffalo shoulder bones fixed to a wooden handle (above). Prior to hoeing, the ground was raked with an antler rake evoking the tale of Everlasting Grandmother whose fields were raked by deer using their horns.

The people of the pueblos separated their corn by color – blue for cornmeal, white for ceremonials, and mixed yellow and red for animal feed. These girls (below) are gathering some grain, possibly in order to bake corn bread in a traditional outdoor oven, or *horno,* introduced by the Spanish.

The centrality of corn in people's lives meant divine forces were credited with its well-being and rituals were evolved to honor their work, maintain the spiritual bond, and keep the rain coming and the soil fertile. Dances and songs – some public, some secret – celebrate the harvest and give thanks.

The fields were first raked free of stalks and other debris from the previous year's crop, difficult roots being prised out of the ground with a digging stick, and then the dried piles of materials were burned, it being recognized that the ashes added to crop yield. The earth was now turned over with a hoe, or digging stick; it was hard, back-breaking work. [41]

Traditionally, tools were of natural materials, the rake made of a portion of deer antlers or bent ash saplings, the hoe from the shoulder bone of a buffalo or other large animal, the heads being lashed to the handle with rawhide strips. Later, metal ones introduced by the traders became popular although some of the older women often preferred to use the traditional tools, biased perhaps by the fact that some tools had sacred associations. The very practical and widely used and ancient digging stick, for example, was represented in the so-called Sacred Woman's Medicine Bundle and also bundles associated with eagle trapping. [42]

The corn was planted on small piles of earth, three or four feet (1-1.3m) apart with several kernels to each pile; beans were frequently planted between the piles. It was not unusual to have a second planting of corn when the 'june-berries were ripe, in order to secure late roasting ears'. [43]

Hidatsa women maintained that it was necessary to be kind to their corn: 'We thought that the corn plants had souls, as children have souls,' said Buffalo Bird Woman. 'We cared for our corn in those days, as we would care for a child'. [44] Buffalo Bird Woman described a typical planting day: 'We Hidatsa women were early risers in the planting season, . . . It was my habit to be up before sunrise, while the air was cool, for we thought this the best time for garden work . . . Planting corn . . . by hand was slow work; but by ten o'clock the morning's work was done, and I was tired and ready to go home for my breakfast and rest'. [45] 'We thought our growing corn liked to hear us sing, just as children like to hear their mothers sing to them,' explained Buffalo Bird Woman. [46]

Such care generally resulted in a bountiful crop and at harvesting time the families held a husking feast. The corn was picked and piled in the field and the next morning, one of the men's societies' criers called the young men to go husking. 'The young men were apt to vie with one another at the husking pile of an attractive girl'. [47] The huskers carefully sorted the corn, most being stacked for threshing. However, particularly good ears were removed to be woven into a braid which generally consisted of 50 or so ears. The selected and braided ears were hung on the corn scaffolds in the village to dry. The soft variegated hues giving the village a gay and festive appearance.

The choice corn was generally parboiled, the grains carefully scraped off the cob and dried in the sun, by laying them on a tanned hide. As one traveler observed, 'Prepared thus, it retains all its juices and flavor and will keep unimpaired almost any length of time. It is then put away in skin bags and carefully hoarded for use on special occasions, or in times of scarcity'. [48] The rest of the

corn was cached: a hole some 6-8ft (2-2.6m) deep was dug in the ground adjacent to or even inside the lodge. The top of the hole was small but it widened out as it deepened. It was lined with hay and the dried corn was then packed in it with more hay and earth on top. Finally, it was carefully trodden down obliterating the site.

Preparation of Maize

Iroquois, Chippewa and other Woodland tribes, frequently cooked fresh maize with beans, meat or other vegetables. They also used popped corn, either whole or ground into a flour and cooked with meat or wild rice. The mature grain was milled raw or parched, the meal being used in various mushes and breads or shaped into cakes or balls. Hominy, particularly popular in the Woodlands, the word deriving from the Algonquian dialects of Virginia or New England, was made by first soaking the grain in a lye of wood ashes to help remove the horny skin; it was then boiled until the skin came off easily.

Less arduous processes used the whole parched corn mixed with dried berries or meat and then pounded into a meal. This in turn was shaped into flat cakes or balls and left to dry.[49] It was a particularly favorite food in the Southwest where it

was referred to as *Pinole*. A variant of this and used in the Woodlands, was a mixture of maple sugar[50] or bear meat with the pounded meal. Preparations of this sort could be stored and left virtually indefinitely; they were particularly popular for use on hunting and warring trips being lightweight, taking up little space and, by the addition of a little water, very nutritious.

Bountiful Resources

There is little question that nature set a bountiful table in many of its cultural areas of North America not only, as we have seen, in plant life, but animal as well; the seas and rivers teemed with seal, otter, whale, salmon, lamprey, halibut, cod, sturgeon, porpoise, trout, herring, haddock, flounder and all varieties of shellfish, while the Woodlands, Plateau, tundra and Plains were the home of big game animals such as moose, wapiti, several varieties of deer, antelope, caribou and buffalo. Bird life also abounded: dominant were the bald and golden eagles, the feathers of the latter being greatly coveted for use in many religious ceremonials.

Much of all this, in various forms, was also used in trade to distant tribes and was often a significant component in the economic wealth of most cultural areas. Thus, it is little wonder that trade routes were well-established long before the white man arrived in North America, together with complex and efficient hunting, as well as gathering, technologies, which exploited the resources of a particular area to a marked degree; such trade and hunting patterns and how they became part of the daily life of the American Indian, are the subject of the next two chapters.[51]

A Hopi man brings in the corn harvest (left). Among the Hopi the women own the fields, their menfolk work them. Men own livestock and fruit trees, but the land in an orchard belongs to women due to their role as clan heads in the matriarchal society.

This Eskimo dish (below) is carved from wood and inlaid with ivory beads. A serving dish, it would probably have been used during ceremonial feasts. The handles are masked human head-forms while the basin itself is decorated with a mythological design.

TRANSPORT AND TRADE

> *'Aboriginal North America was blanketed by a network of trails and trading relationships linking, to a greater or lesser degree, every tribe to one or more of its neighbors. That is, every North American group engaged in trade with some of its neighbors . . . This network functioned very efficiently in moving goods across the continent . . .'*
>
> WOOD AND LIBERTY [1]

FROM TIME IMMEMORIAL, American Indians were well familiar with places hundreds, perhaps even thousands, of miles distant from one another, a main stimulus for this interaction being the acquisition of highly-prized trade commodities such as marine shells, obsidian, and turquoise which 'traveled hundreds and in some cases, thousands of miles from their origins'.[2] Countless trade centers existed where distant tribes could meet and exchange goods and these centers were linked together by a complex network of trade routes which were in almost continual use.

Waterways and Trails

Transportation, particularly in the Northeast and on the west coast, was often by boat, traversing the rivers and streams or putting out to sea. In the Northeast, where perhaps more than anywhere the traders followed the water courses, the 'carry' or 'portage' was frequently resorted to. Here, the boat was unloaded to get past obstructions and both cargo and the lightweight birch bark canoe were carried between the different waterways. In contrast, to the south, and below the birch bark line where boats were invariably of the dugout type and hence heavy, the concept of portage was virtually unknown. In addition to the waterways were extensive paths and trails, many formed by the movements of large animals – deer,

moose, buffalo – in their seasonal migrations or quest for food and water.[3] Often these paths were in such frequent use that the ground was packed and vegetation sparse, defining trails which could be hundreds of miles in extent. 'Many maps of the colonial period, supplemented by other records, indicate that these ways of communication extended with few breaks practically the entire length and breadth of the continent'.[4] Travel along such routes was always on foot and in single file and while many trails seldom exceeded 1ft 6in (50cm) in width, with appropriate planning they adequately satisfied the requirements of travel for generations of traders, migrating bands, war parties, hunters and ambassadors of peace. Goods were carried in back packs of tough buckskin, rolled tightly to enable swift, unimpeded movements.

Prisoners and Wounded

The narrowness of these trails, however, demanded considerable ingenuity if they were to be effectively used, particularly in times of war. Thus, prisoners' hands were bound at the front and restrained by belts tied around the neck, waist and arms. They were made to walk ahead and carry a gourd rattle so their presence and location were always apparent. Wounded or sick members of the party presented particular problems and their comfort was of least consideration. The French explorer, Samuel Champlain (1615), who accompanied a retreating Huron war party, gives us some interesting insights into this aspect

The greatest change to Indian methods of transportation occured with the introduction of the horse by the Spanish. The horse travelers of the Plains used the travois to take their goods with them from camp to camp. These Gros Ventre (main picture) are carrying parfleches on their travois. The travois consisted of two lodge-pole pines which crossed over the horse's back and had a small platform between. The horse also became another good to be traded – or captured. Intertribal trade networks were very extensive, the goods ranging from raw materials, such as dentalium shell (right and far left), to finished, manufactured items such as pottery . This jar (above left) was made in the pueblos of the Southwest, pottery and suchlike being traded at places like Pecos or Taos where the settled Rio Grande farmers could barter with the nomads from the Plains and Plateau.

The birch bark canoe was a skilfully crafted item which came in a variety of forms - some quite distinctive to particular tribes (the Ottowa, for example, favored a high prow and stern). It was the ideal transport with which to negotiate the northern waterways. These low-ended Ojibwa canoes (above) were the most efficient types in calm waters.

Moccasins were a comfortable form of footwear and enabled quiet movement through the forest, although they might not endure a rough terrain too well. These Huron examples (right) have been decorated with trade-acquired wool cloth, silk ribbon and beads to enhance the traditional moosehair embroidery.

of northeastern Indian life. Preparing for an 800 mile (1,287km) journey back to Huronia, the Huron spent considerable time making 'curious harnesses for the transport of the wounded [which]. . . resembled the carrying frames for papooses', being a frame of wood which rested against the carrier's back with a small seat projecting at right angles. The frame was held in place by straps of hide or inner elm bark cords and partially supported by a tump-line over the carrier's forehead. 'The wounded man sat on the precarious seat, his back to the bearer's back. His legs were hunched under his chin and tightly bound in an intolerable position'.[5] Champlain himself, immobilized by two Iroquois arrow wounds in his leg, was one of a number carried this way: he was 'tossed and buffeted, helpless, on his bearer's back, whipped by branches, beaten by snow, [and] half immersed in forded streams'.[6] Little wonder that, as soon as he gained strength to stand, he quickly 'got out of that prison, or rather hell'.[7] Nevertheless, such parties, even so encumbered, could move rapidly on foot along these well worn routes and Champlain's companions covered 60 miles (96km) in just two days.[8]

The Good Trail

Several factors made for a good trail in the Woodlands: obviously, the routes of least natural resistance were generally followed. However, rough terrain was avoided where possible since this rapidly wore away the soft-soled moccasins

so characteristic of the region.[9] War parties generally followed routes selected by the scouts, animal trails often being followed; dense brush and thickets were avoided as these impeded progress and reduced stealth; using the bed of a stream for some way helped obliterate tracks and confuse the enemy. Many of the trails ran along high ground where the undergrowth was relatively sparse, the soil drained and dried quickly, and streams were few and shallow.

Assessing the Enemy

Universal was the concern of avoiding the enemy, assessing their strength and gaining positions of advantage for any possible encounter. Eons of experience enabled much to be learned from deserted camp sites; typical is that reported for the Assiniboin (Plains) by the experienced fur trader, Edwin Denig:

'The camp fires will show how many persons have slept there, the dung of the horses or dogs denotes the time, if the fires have become cool. The tracks of the men and animals and the remains of the meal are also means of judging. If scraps of meat or bone seen around are untouched by wolves or ravens, they must conclude that the party has recently left . . . In summer the bending of the grass under their feet, tracks in crossing a stream or any marshy place, and in winter, tracks in the snow, will show a tolerable certainty how many persons and what time they have passed. A slight rain would determine whether the tracks were before or since it fell. . . A correct judgement is not, however, formed by any one of the above criterions, but by a comparison of the whole, and by following the trail, and observing also the carcases of the animals killed by the party, their number, state of decay, etc. These with other smaller indications, particularly if an arrow or moccasin be lost or thrown away, will determine the number and nation that have passed and the time . . . .'.[10]

Acute Senses

While the physical anthropologist, Ales Hrdlicka was of the opinion that the 'ordinary' Indian with healthy eyes and ears possessed very good faculties of sight and hearing, he concluded that it was 'no way phenomenal'.[11] This observation differs sharply from that of Edwin Denig who, in 1854, recorded that Plains Indians had an 'extreme acuteness in their sense of sight' and that Indians

Tom Lovell's painting The Wolf Men depicts Comanche scouts covering their war party's tracks from the keen eyes of their enemies in whose territory they are raiding. The wolf was revered for its keen senses and avoidance of pursuers.

This Bering Strait Inuit sled (right) is a particularly large one with many more dogs than the usual three or four. The husky dogs were the only domestic animal used by the peoples of the far north and they had done so for thousands of years. The husky not only pulled the sled but with its keen sense of smell it helped locate seals . The sled's runners were usually made from whale bones or caribou antlers.

possessed a remarkable ability to distinguish between various types of animals – horses, buffalo, elk, antelope, bear, wolf, deer, pick out men up to 15 miles (24km) away and the 'greatest mystery' was that

'they make out anything living to be there at such a distance, on the instant, when they themselves are in motion and the animal at rest. . . . [then] the movements are watched and its character thus determined. . . . they also judge very correctly the relative distances of objects, either by eye or to each other . . . Their ideas of location are fully as remarkable'.[12]

The same writer reports the remarkable ability of the Indians he observed, to find discharged arrows 'whereas a white man would have trouble in finding any one [of them]': additionally, lost objects or animals, and hidden camps, were located with relative ease 'even if they have never been in the neighborhood of the place'.[13]

Good trails, acute senses and physical stamina, however, were insufficient to give a high degree of camp mobility and various forms of ingenious modes of transportation were devised in several cultural areas. Paramount as the pioneers of fast

travel were the Arctic peoples who used, in addition to the *kayak*, skin boat and, on occasions, the bark canoe, a sled pulled by dogs.

The Sled

Sleds differed considerably in shape and construction being dependent on the nature of the terrain to be traversed and the materials available; generally, however, they were of uniform widths to enable the same tracks to be followed and, owing to the adverse effects of the frost and the unusual amounts of strain, neither pegs nor nails were used. Instead, various parts of the sled runners, the bed, back and front rests, braces and guide bars, were lashed together with rawhide thongs, a wide variety of ties and knots being employed. In areas where wood was scarce, sled runners were often of bone, ingeniously cut, shaped and then sewn together with thin thongs or heavy sinew. These runners were then shoed with short strips of ivory or carefully selected smooth bone and generally held in place with countersunk thongs to avoid unraveling. The main types of sleds were low and flat without a rail, which could be used to transport *umiaks*[14] and bulky objects, while a built-up sled having a high rail on each side was used for transporting camp equipment and loads of smaller articles. To reduce friction to a minimum, the shoes and runners were often coated with a mixture of blood and salt or coated with a layer of smooth ice. Dogs were harnessed either in a single or fanwise trace; the Alaskan Eskimo generally used lines of tough walrus hide and on occasions a bitch on heat was used as a lead dog 'so that the other dogs would follow more readily'.[15] However, lead dogs were generally carefully trained; they became household pets and were kept inside during the winter and not staked out in the snow as were the other members of the team. Such animals responded to the calls of the driver, the other dogs following. 'The dog stops on command and has learnt to change direction, either at verbal command or when the driver exclaims, '*mawna, mawna!*' (turn!] and indicates the direction with his arm. The dog in the latter case will stop and look behind to note the direction indicated by the driver . . .'.[16]

The Snowshoe

It is highly probable that the snowshoe was an Old World invention, its introduction to the Arctic and Subarctic regions having a comparable influence on the indigenous peoples as did the introduction of the horse by the Spanish to the Plateau and Plains tribes farther south. The 'snowshoe complex' it has been suggested, was initially adopted by the Alaskan and Yukon Athapaskan groups enabling an inland culture to occupy the entire length and breadth of the northern boreal forests, the exploitative advantage of the snowshoe rendering rapid and efficient movement over otherwise impassable snow or very soft ground.[17]

The main parts of the snowshoe are the wooden frame with a toe and heel crossbar, generally of wood but sometimes of rawhide. In addition, there might be extra strengthening bars and a complex webbing of thin rawhide strips, generally referred to by the French as *babiche*.[18] The size of the webbing varied considerably, a coarser web being used for soft wet snow; shapes also differed, each designed to best suit the terrain and snow density. Generally, they were long and narrow in the west, while among the Montagnais-Naskapi in the east, they were much broader, some oval, and others almost round. The shape often determined the name used to describe a particular style of snowshoe – Swallowtail, Bear Paw and Beaver Tail being some common terms.

Putting on the snowshoe and subsequently walking, required considerable skill. The hands were not used, the foot being thrust through the ankle loop after which, by a clever twist, the toe was positioned under the loop itself. Walking was accomplished with a long and swinging stride, the toe being lifted while the heel was left to drag.

This pair of snowshoes and a snow walking stick (above) are from the Carrier of British Columbia. Note the distinctive upturned toes on the shoes and the pattern on the stick known as burned spiral design.

This Ojibwa hunter (left) wears snowshoes in order to be able to pursue deer or moose across the snowy terrain. The animals were slowed down by the snow but the hunter was greatly assisted by his snowshoes and could cover 50 miles (80km) a day.

This snowshoe (above) is from the Naskapi and is much rounder in shape when compared to the longer, narrower Carrier example shown on the previous page.

Prior to the introduction of the horse the dog was the only beast of burden available to the Plains Indians. It could pull a reasonable load on a travois (right) but it was not very reliable or efficient, being distracted easily by other dogs and smaller animals such as rabbits which it liked to chase if the opportunity presented itself! Dogs were still used to drag firewood after the horse was introduced and men might also take them hunting.

While most highly developed by – and essential to – the Arctic and Subarctic peoples, the snowshoe was by no means exclusive to these cultural areas. Thus, in the Pacific states of Washington and California, the rim of the snowshoe was round or slightly oval, the heel and toe bar were replaced with a heavy rawhide rope and the webbing was of an open, simple kind. East to the Nez Perce on the Plateau, snowshoes were generally oval in shape having a frame of vine maple or hackberry with strips of elk rawhide. Unlike those to the north, the webbing was not cross-woven but was a 'loop mesh made somewhat after the manner of the sewing thread in coiled basketry. . . . a single strip was woven in loops from the outside to the center. A second and a third strip followed till the mesh became small enough'.[19] These snowshoes were generally strapped tightly to the foot and, unlike in the Arctic and Subarctic regions, they were lifted bod-

ily when walking; the snowshoe in this region was commonly worn in hunting deer in winter. Deep winter snow on the Great Plains also led to considerable use of the snowshoe. George Catlin, for example, illustrates a Sioux pair, 'which are used in deep snows of the winter, under the Indians feet, to buoy him up as he runs in pursuit of his game'.[20]

Mandan snowshoes, apparently, differed somewhat from most styles if the pair collected by Maximilian are typical of the tribe. Here, the webbing, instead of the usual *babiche*, is of buckskin strips over a wooden frame, the long tie straps and position of the toe and heel supports, suggest that they were, as with the Nez Perce, lifted bodily when walking.[21]

The Dog and Horse

Like the Eskimo, the early Plains Indians also commonly used dogs for transportation. Instead of the sled, a travois was drawn by the dog; this simple wheel-less device consisted of two poles for side pieces which crossed over the back of the

One reason the dog found the travois difficult to pull was the resistance offered by the weighed-down poles as they dragged across the rough country. Even then, however, it could manage 6 miles (10km) a day with a 70lbs (32kg) load. Obviously the horse ('big dog' to the Cree) found this a great deal less of a problem, although even then the poles and cover of a typical lodge was of sufficient weight to require two horses to transport it. A small Cheyenne child was less of a problem (left). Working normally a horse could manage 40 miles (64km) with up to a 300lbs (136kg) load.

animal. The poles supported a central rest made of a netted rawhide circular hoop or rectangular frame and the butt ends dragged along the ground. Strong dogs could themselves carry a load of about 50lbs (23kg) but the use of the travois increased efficiency by some 50 percent, Ewers estimating that some 75lbs (34kg) could then be transported.[22]

It is obvious that the limit on loading considerably reduced the nomadism of the Plains tribes prior to the introduction of the horse; indeed, to supplement the dog transport, the women were also obliged to carry heavy loads on their backs and dog transport was inadequate for conveying children, aged or sick people. Blackfeet informants were of the opinion that a 'train of heavily loaded dogs would travel no more than five or six miles a day'.[23]

With the establishment of Spanish rule in New Mexico by Juan de Onate, circa 1600, several hundred horses were imported from the Old

Very often there was nothing to replace human power - more often than not that meant woman power. This Apache burden basket (left) is lightweight and made of willow and devil's claw decorated with leather fringe and metal tinklers. It was carried on the back and used to transport grain, firewood and personal goods.

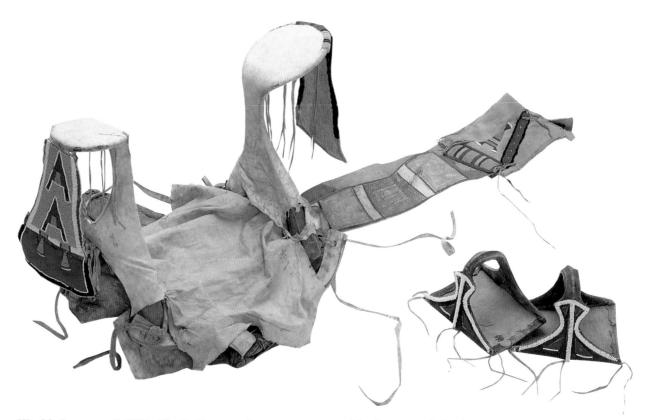

In terms of horses, the Crow were the richest tribe on the central Plains, exceeded in the Plains' region as a whole only by the Comanche and the Fort Sill Apache in the late-19th century. The horse culture produced an array of equipment, much of it brilliantly and distinctively decorated. This Crow woman's saddle and stirrups (right) were collected in the 1890s. The beaded high pommel and cantle marks this out as Crow and belonging to the wife of a notable man. Men tended to favor less elaborate horse gear.

World. By around 1650, Ute Indians – who occupied the eastern Great Basin cultural area and forayed into the southern Plains region and followed the buffalo – were described as using pack horses (as well as the dog travois), although apparently at this time they did not ride the horse. The Pueblo Revolt of 1680 led to an additional rich source of horses from the Eastern Pueblos and by the early 1700s the Shoshoni and Comanche extended their hunting range as far as the South Saskatchewan River in Canada to the Red River in present-day Manitoba and North Dakota. The Shoshoni-Comanche dominance of the central and northern Plains, however, was short lived as the Blackfeet, Cree and other previously pedestrian tribes acquired not only the horse but also guns and metal weapons from white sources to the east. By around 1750, Shoshonians had been forced west and south and the equestrian culture was progressively developed by such tribes as the Blackfeet, Cree, Sarsi and Crow, later joined by the Sioux, Cheyenne and Arapaho.[24]

The impact of the horse on the daily life of a typical Plains tribe – the Blackfeet – was immense. Not only did the acquisition of the horse enable faster and farther camp movement but much greater loads could be carried; as Ewers observed:

'The horse, packing 200 pounds on its back or hauling 300 pounds on the travois could move four times the load of a heavily burdened dog twice as far in a day's march. Thus, animal for animal the horse was eight times as efficient as the dog as a burden bearer. Horse transport permitted the manufacture, use, and movement of lodges with larger and heavier covers and longer poles – larger homes. . . . Women no longer were compelled to carry backbreaking burdens . . . The aged and the physically handicapped could be carried on travois, and were no longer in danger of abandonment on the Plains by their able bodied fellows'.[25]

The introduction of the horse not only brought a dramatic change in daily life, material culture and hunting and warfare patterns but the spiritual world views were also notably influenced. Thus, ancient traditions and rituals were adjusted to the changed conditions and a wealth

These Crow girls (left) look elegant in their elk tooth dresses mounted astride their richly embellished horses. Note the decor of the cruppers, collars and headstalls. Plains children were taught to ride at an early age and most were quite proficient by the age of six or seven.

of new myths and ceremonial associated with the horse extended symbolic concepts and ritual. Further, horse embellishment became increasingly more elaborate; often the accoutrements were more than merely practical, much being replete in symbolic statements. Throughout the Plains, Plateau and beyond, the horse was considered a great marvel and frequently regarded as sacred or having a mysterious character. Many tribes explained its origin by elaborate myths which referred to the horse as emerging from the sun, lakes, springs or the earth. When the Spanish explorers visited the Hopi in 1583, they spread kilts and scarfs on the ground for the horses to walk on in the belief that they were sacred. As Grinnell has observed, 'This sacred character is sometimes shown in the names given to the horse, such as the Lakota *sunka wakan*, 'mysterious dog'. Its use in transportation accounts for the term 'dog' often applied to it, as the *Siksika ponokamita*, 'elk dog'; Cree *mistatim*, 'big dog"; and Shawnee *mishawa*, 'elk'.[26]

Wealth in horses greatly increased a man's standing; one exceptional individual in this respect – although it was a pattern replicated throughout the Plains, Plateau and beyond albeit

generally on a smaller scale – was the head chief of the Piegan (Blackfeet), 'Many Horses'. This man was particularly noted for the very large number of horses which he acquired by capturing them from the Shoshoni and also breeding them as soon as the first were obtained from the Kutenai in the early 1800s. Eventually his horse herd became so large that they outnumbered all the others belonging to the Piegan and ultimately 'He had so many horses he could not keep track of them all!'[27]

The Sign Language and Signals

As has already been discussed, centuries before Euroamerican penetration, American Indians had established extensive trade networks across North America.[28] These contacts between many different linguistic groups demanded an efficient way of communication and while more specialised vocal communication such as the Chinook jargon was used in trade interactions in the

Soapstone was one of the precious commodities traded widely across the continent. This Huron effigy pipe bowl was carved from soapstone acquired from the Arctic region to the north and west. The Virginian tobacco smoked in the Arctic pipes was obtained by the Eskimos from Russian traders.

The fur trade brought about imense activity between Indian tribes and European traders. The sign language was an important and effective means of communicating across language barriers, a vital skill to enable what were frequently complex transactions to take place. In addition, mixed-blood Ojibwa-French *Metis* acted as mediators and interpreters.

northwest, a widely used system was that of signs.

Communication by signs was ancient and widespread. Thus, in 1528 when Cabeca de Vaca traveled to the region of Tampa Bay in present-day Florida and in his subsequent journeying through Texas and Mexico, he reported that although he encountered many different tongues, he communicated effectively in signs 'Just as if they spoke our language and we theirs'. There is also some evidence which suggests extensive and early use of gesture signs by the Iroquoian and Algonquian tribes of the Northeast although as Tomkins has observed, there was a gradual 'decadence of signs'

arising from a wide 'acquaintance with the English language'.[29]

Little Raven, a Southern Arapaho chief, summed up the widespread use of sign language:

'I have met . . . tribes whose vocal language we did not understand, but we communicated freely in sign language . . . the summer after President Lincoln was killed we had a grand gathering of all the tribes to the east and south of us. Twenty-five different tribes met near old Fort Abercrombie on the Wichita River. The Caddo had a different sign for horse, and also for moving, but the rest were made the same for all the tribes'.[30]

Extensive contacts with Plains Indians during the 19th century enabled detailed studies to be made of the use of sign language and its extensive and important use among many linguistically unrelated groups.[31] The grace and beauty of the sign language, where skilled individuals could communicate three times faster than they could speak, led one scholar to observe

'In fluent grace of movement a conversation in the sign language between a Cheyenne and a Kiowa is the very poetry of motion . . . each tribe is designated by a special sign combination '. . . thus "Blackfoot" is indicated by the speaker touching his moccasin and then rubbing "his fingers upon something black" . . . for Pawnee, the "Wolf people" the sign talker "throws up his right hand, with two fingers apart and pointing upward and forward, at the side of his head, to indicate erect ears of a wolf, following this with a sign for man . . ." '.

Some signs, the same scholar reported were 'beautifully symbolic'. Thus, 'fatigue' was shown by a downward and outward sweep of the two hands in front of the body, index fingers extended, giving a gesture – picture of utter collapse. 'Bad' was indicated by a motion of throwing away;

'truth' by signs for straight talk, and 'falsehood' by the talk sign, with another for different directions, that is 'talking two ways'.[32]

In addition to the sign language, the American Indians also developed an extensive signal system to enable communication between groups while on hunting or war expeditions. This was achieved by the waving of a robe or blanket, riding in a particular way or by smoke signals. In this way, location of game, the advice to advance or retreat, the number of enemy seen or losses sustained was conveyed to distant parties.

Many of the signals were extensions of the sign language but on a larger scale. The nature of the signal was determined by the terrain; in open country such as on the Plains, regions of the Plateau, the Southwest and on the clear beaches of Florida, arm, blanket and movement signals could easily be seen whereas in the forests of the Northeast and along the misty shores of the Northwest Coast, such modes of communication were limited, auditory – drum and calls – signals being used.

Smoke and Other Signals

Smoke signals were employed over a wide area west of the Mississippi and into the Plateau region. The fire was generally built on a high ele-

Howard Terpning's painting Signals in the Wind (below) portrays a smoke signal scene from the viewpoint of the Blackfeet party observing it. Here the winter wind is dispersing the signal but they will know what it means because, like most signals, it would follow a code that had been agreed shortly beforehand.

vation, heavy smoke being produced by use of green leaves or damp grass. While smoke signals were not such a standardized code as the sign language, there were definite signals recognized by various tribes. Thus, returning Pima war parties, as well as other tribes in the region such as the Papago and Apache, generally gave advance notice of the number of scalps taken by means of a corresponding number of fires lit within view of the home village; returning Omaha war parties, if successful, kindled a fire when within sight of the village, the rising smoke giving the signal of the victorious return of the warriors.[33] The explorer, Jean Louis Berlandier, who in the late-1820s traveled among the Indians of Texas, was obviously much impressed by the efficiency of communication at a distance between the various tribes of the region, recording

'Their telegraphs, by means of which they communicate over immense distances, are certainly no product of the instinct. Almost all the peoples of these deserts use fires, with various devices to allow the smoke to escape in puffs, or spread, or do something else, to announce to their allies or to the rest of their nation a victory, a trail, a meeting, the route of the enemy, or whatever else they wish to communicate'.[34]

Additionally, motion signals were made either on foot or horse, the robe or blanket often being used, described as 'frequently extremely picturesque in execution'.[35] Thus, the signal for 'buffalo' was made by holding the open robe or blanket at two corners with the arms outstretched above the head and then gracefully bringing it down toward the ground. The signal for 'enemy' was made by rapidly waving the outstretched robe several times above the head; this was similar to the 'all clear' signal of the Omaha when the robe was gently waved from side to side in front of the body, while their 'alarm' signal was executed by throwing the robe into the air several times in rapid succession.[36]

With the introduction of mirrors, several Plains tribes – particularly the Sioux – developed a system of heliograph signals, communicating over considerable distances, even conveying information to moving war parties.[37]

Maps and Map-making

The extensive traveling which we know American Indians did on their trading expeditions throughout the American continent, and indeed sometimes even beyond,[38] required an intimate knowledge of the geography of the country through which they were to pass and the value of maps to facilitate this was widely recognized.

While in later years, with increased contact with Euroamericans, indigenous mapping techniques were modified, many of the essential features were retained. Thus, straight lines and smooth curves usually referred to linkages between points and did not necessarily represent route details. In this respect, one scholar has recently observed, 'Indian maps had much more in common with modern public-transport-user guides than with topographic maps'.[39]

Map-making techniques are obviously ancient in North America; indeed, there is some evidence to suggest that simple cartographic principles were incorporated in several of the prehistoric rock art sites which have been documented across the Great Plains and beyond.[40] One of the earliest references to map-making techniques is probably that of Jacques Cartier (1491-1557) who obtained from Algonquian Indians, information relating to the course of the St. Lawrence which they delineated 'with certaine little stickes which they layde upon the ground in a certaine distance, and afterwards layde other small

branches between both representing the Saults'.[41]

In the early 1700s, the Jesuit missionary Lafitau reported that the Iroquois made 'exact maps' which he said they kept in their public treasury to consult them at need'.[42] In later years, explorers, travelers, traders and military men refer to the indigenous use of maps throughout all the cultural areas of North America, including the Northwest Coast tribes.[43] These maps were used, among other activities, to plan war expeditions and to communicate with each other on journeys, such as trade and hunting expeditions; they were also employed in religious ceremonials such as the famous star chart of the Skidi Pawnee. Indeed, maps and mapping techniques, it has been observed, were so much part of the daily life of American Indians in structuring their world 'that they actually *dream* maps'.[44]

The Southern Ojibwa retained sacred scrolls which were kept with the accoutrements associated with the *Midewiwin* Society of the tribe. These were engraved birch bark sheets some of which have been very convincingly interpreted as migration charts, representing in a cartographic form the route by which the Ojibwa people believed that they received the

The carving of rare argillite stone – extracted from a mountain in the Queen Charlotte Islands – offers an example of an Indian craft developed mainly to cater to a European desire for native curios. This superb Haida chest was carved by the famous Charles Edenshaw. The Haida began the art in about 1820 and by 1880 they were introducing concepts that might wel have been taboo in traditional art. This chest incorporates bold images of tribal mythology such as the chestlid figure of raven, the trickster and cultural hero, but depicted here with both human and birdlike attributes.

Midewiwin religion. Reference is made to the 'Great Salt Water' (The Atlantic Ocean), the St. Lawrence, then through the Great Lakes following the head of Lake Superior to Leech Lake in central Minnesota. Although highly schematic, and touching on a number of mythical events, the charts can be related to the Great Lakes-St. Lawrence drainage system, the interpretation of which was retained in the oral history of the tribe.

Migration maps of this type do not appear to be unique; the *Walam Olum* touches on such concepts and, more positively, a map kept by an early Mandan chief, Good Furred Robe, was said to document the migration of the tribe to their location in present-day North Dakota, via the Mississippi and Missouri waterways from the remote south which may have extended to the Gulf of Mexico.[45] Such cultural documents were, almost daily, referred to by tribal historians in relating the oral history of the tribe.[46]

Intertribal Trade

As has already been discussed, archeological evidence and oral history indicate that long before the white man set foot in North America there was a well-established network of trade relationships with major trade centers generally located 'among sedentary native populations with surplus-abundant economies [which were] able to selectively harvest and trade food and other commodities to non-horticultural and fellow farming or fishing neighbours'.[47] In the Southwest, for example, the Spaniards who arrived early in the 16th century found that the pueblos of Taos, Zuni, Pecos and Hopi were vibrant with multiethnic trade activity, with trade routes which extended to the Great Plains, Basin, Plateau, California and south into Mexico. Similar activity was observed by early Russian (circa 1780) and English traders who sailed to the Northwest Coast. Tlingit, Nootka, Makah, Chinook, Yurok,

The Chilkat blanket of the Tlingit was a popular trade piece, but the ones used for trade were sometimes inferior versions using poor wools and methods. The best authentic blankets were complicated pieces to produce and might take up to six months to complete, being woven by a woman to the design of her husband or father. Any Tlingit man that could afford to pay the high fee required for the work was therefore a wealthy man worthy of considerable respect. The blankets offered conventionalized mythological representations in a unilaterally symmetrical style; that shown here (right) is described as a diving whale design.

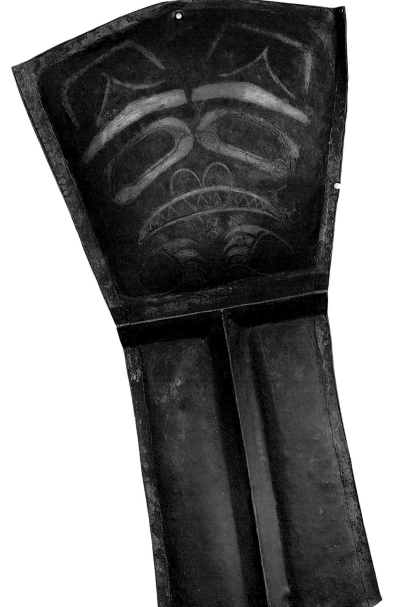

hair, 'ermine skins, native copper, plates, and spruce-root baskets from the Tlingit; dugout cedar canoes from the Haida; mountain goat horn spoons, Raven rattles, dance headdresses, and eulachon oil from the Tsimshian; mountain goat hair and horn from the Bella Coola. . . dentalium shells were one of the most popular and widespread commodities, they were especially prized by the Yurok, who used them as money'.[48]

While relatively isolated from the rest of North America by the Cascade and other mountain ranges to the east, rivers which cut through the massive mountain walls enabled important trade links to be established. In particular, Chinookans (hence 'Chinook jargon') brought west coast trade goods to The Dalles, obtaining in return, native tobacco, baskets and bags, buffalo robes, even horses and slaves from such tribes as the Nez Perce and Cayuse. In turn, the Plateau tribes forged links with the Mountain Crow, and by a complex link of secondary trade centers or rendezvous, transported native and European trade goods across the Great Plains and Woodlands in the east.[49]

This superb ivory pipe (above) carries its own cleaner attached to the top. The Eskimo generally traded such fine pieces. Those for everyday use were far less elaborate.

Copper had great value among the Northwest Coast tribes. Coppers, such as the Kwakiutl one seen here (above left), might have a value of several thousand Hudson's Bay blankets. Coppers were rare items and greatly treasured possessions. They were engraved on a black background in the form of a conventionalized face representing the crest animal of the owner – in this example it is a bear.

Pomo and Shasta carried on a lively trade which extended north to Bristol Bay on the Alaskan Peninsula, south to northern California and east to the great Dalles trade center on the Columbia River, Washington. The reverberations of this, via secondary trade centers, were felt at the Mandan, Hidatsa, Arikara, Pawnee, Wichita and Caddo villages on the eastern Plains, more than 2,000 miles (3,218km) away.

Both specialized and rare commodities were traded along the coast and east to The Dalles; some were exotic goods, others of a more practical nature. Thus, Chilkat blankets of goat and dog

THE HUNT AND WAR

'We knew the habits of the different kinds of birds and that each kind had its own feeding grounds where we would find them.'

GOODBIRD (HIDATSA) [1]

ALL HUNTERS, OF COURSE, need to be well-versed in a variety of processes and the North American Indians were no exception. Paramount was the selection of the appropriate traps or weapons but in addition a knowledge of the quarry's behavioral patterns, the use of decoys, calls, whistles, clothing, shelters and hiding places, and of the food to eat together with any associated taboos, were all vital to ensure success. A knowledge, too, of the hunting rituals and ceremonials together with their songs and fetishes, were also the requirements of any successful hunter.

There was also a variety of associated activities and skills. Thus, in order to hunt a buffalo with the bow, it was necessary to have a well-trained buffalo horse; or to spear a moose in deep snow (a commonly-used technique), the efficient use of snowshoes was needed.

All these attributes and more, together produced skilled and perceptive individuals who alone, but more often by cooperative effort, achieved a high degree of success in the hunting process.

Hunting Like a Man

Widespread was the practice of boys being taught how to hunt and trap by their fathers, older relatives or a trusted family friend; their roles as hunters were thus conditioned from an early age. Typical are the experiences of the Hidatsa men,

Wolf Chief and Goodbird, who related the days of their youths to the anthropologist Gilbert Wilson. Wolf Chief told of his early use of the bow and arrow: 'I began using a bow, I think, when I was four years of age . . . I very often went out to hunt birds for so my father bade me do'. Armed with blunt arrows and snares, the Hidatsa boys learned skills they would need as hunters and warriors. Goodbird gave more details:

'[My] bow was made of choke cherry wood and was a little longer than the arrows. The latter were made of buck-brush shoots . . . With such arrows I was allowed to shoot around in the lodge as they were thought too light to do any damage.'[2]

From older companions – such as Goodbird above – the boys learned all the important lessons for successful hunting, knowing the prey and having the right equipment. The boys also learned which types of arrows flew best, what feathers were the best for fletching and how to avoid them getting lost in the grass. They were taught, too, the rules of generosity which prevailed on the hunting expeditions.

'If I went in a party of three or four boys, the bird belonged, not to the one who killed it, but to the one who picked it up. And if I shot a bird, I would call out, "Heh, – I have shot a bird. Come and find it!" And all the others would run. When an older and more skillful

The abilities to hunt and to wage war were essential masculine attributes in most of indigenous North America. Indeed, for some tribes warfare was central to their culture and individuals gained enormous respect and stature in their society by their warrior exploits. The Sioux were one such tribe and a man like Kicking Bear (left, main picture), of the Miniconjou band, was a prime example of a high status warrior distinguished for his deeds in battle. A warrior-hunter, of course, required the accoutrements of his 'profession' and these ranged from clothing to adornment to tools and weaponry (the border, right and far left, is from the shaft of a war club). A warrior's status might be indicated by elements of clothing, or perhaps by a symbolic carving such as that shown here (above left) used by a Piegan warrior to mark his place during council meetings.

87

This wood and ivory float rack (right) had a practical purpose, serving to keep harpoons, spears, floats and lines in place on a *kayak*. The beautiful figurines of small seals that decorate it also serve another purpose as magical aids to invoke success in the hunt.

This Tlingit harpoon head and line (below) dates from the 1890s. This head has a metal point with bone; a traditionally made spear or attachment might have had a point of mussel shell with added bone spurs or barbs.

boy went out as partner to another, the more skillful boy might get no birds at all, because all his kill would go to his partner'.[3]

Hunting, however, was recognized as a dangerous occupation. Wolf Chief described one particularly disastrous expedition which he made with his father in the winter. On this trip Wolf Chief went snowblind, was almost suffocated when he climbed into a porcupine's den and nearly froze in a sudden blizzard! 'But the camaraderie he shared with his father made up for many hardships'.[4]

A widespread custom was the celebration of a young hunter's first successful kill. Typical was that of the Chippewa's 'Feast of the First Game'. Here, all the village was invited by the boy's parents, the meat of the animal killed being served as part of the main dish. As one Chippewa lady recalled, 'When my brother caught his first deer, and later his bear, my mother prepared the animal – head, hoofs and insides – and invited all the old people'.[5] At such feasts, it was usual for one of the older and respected men to make a speech, appealing to the *manidog*, 'the spirits', so that the boy would continue being successful as he grew older.

The Nootkan Whale Hunt

Of all hunts for big game carried out by the North American Indians, perhaps among the most spectacular, dramatic and daring, was the whale hunt of the Nootka, a powerful seafaring tribe of

Vancouver Island's west coast. These people, together with the related Makah, Quinault and Quileute, had a particular reputation as brave and highly skilled whalers who in 30ft (10m) dugout canoes and led by a hereditary chief – whaling was considered the noblest calling – hunted the great humpback and gray whales which, in the spring and summer, were abundant along the shores and inlets of Nootka territory.

Preparation for the hunt, as in several other cultural areas, involved the leader in extensive training and ritual, often extending over several months 'bathing and scouring his body, praying, and swimming in imitation of actions desired in the whale, his wife holding him on a line'.[6] Likewise, the seven crew members, a steersman and six paddlers, also underwent considerable preparation and were ritually administered for the dangers ahead.

The leader acted as the harpooner and occupied a position in the bow of the canoe. The whaling gear was assembled when they reached the hunting grounds, consisting of sealskin floats, coils of cedar-withe rope and various sharp, pointed and chisel-headed lances for crippling the wounded whale and for the final kill, but the the leader's harpoon was the most significant of the equipment used, being some 18ft (6m) in length.

A whaling expedition usually comprised the whaler and his crew accompanied by two or three other canoes with junior relatives and their crews. A calm, windless day was preferred for the

hunt and 'when a whale was sighted, the lead canoe was swiftly and quietly manoeuvred into striking position on the whale's left side. The harpooner stood in the bow. . . holding the armed harpoon shaft almost horizontally above his shoulders'.[7] Then perhaps he prayed:

'Whale, when I spear you, I want
my spear to strike your heart. Harpoon,
when I throw you, I want you to go to the
heart of the whale.[8]

The 'strike was made just as the whale began to sound. The harpooner plunged the harpoon into the cetacean's left side, striking just behind the flipper'.[9] It was vital that the strike was exactly on the right spot and occurred just as the whale was submerging; any other situation could be disastrous and it took great patience and skill to satisfy these conditions. After the successful hit and the whale had resurfaced, the other canoes approached, the men now plunging more harpoons into the animal's body. The exhausted whale was finally dispatched with a pointed

This Ingalik man (left) from the Subarctic is removing fish from his trap using a wooden scoop (in his left hand). Traps of this type were commonly used to catch ling. Behind him, upright in the snow and ice, is an ice chisel and a long wooden ice scoop. Hunters often took their young sons along to educate them in the ways of hunting.

This wooden dish (below) was collected from the Haida of Cape Masset in 1893. It features both an eagle and a whale in a deliberate visual pun. The panel between the two heads has been carved to look like a whale's pectoral fin and an eagle's curving wing.

The use of an *atlatl* gave the hunter's throwing arm an extra joint and enabled him to project the harpoon further and with greater force. This Bering Strait Inuit man (right) is using an *atlatl* to throw with from his one-hole *kayak*.

This superbly executed drag handle of carved ivory (right) represents a seal rising to the surface to breathe. At the top a smaller seal has already broken the water's surface to look around.

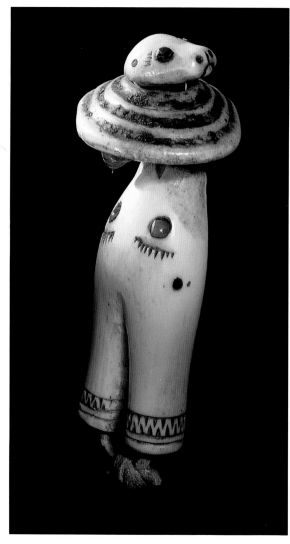

lance: it was a frightening, bloody and brutal struggle.

When dead, the whale's jaws were lashed tightly shut to keep it afloat and additional seal floats were tied to the carcass. Now the long hard task of towing the whale home began, several of the canoes being used. Amidst a great ceremonial welcome, the carcass was finally beached, the people singing the ancient whale songs:

'I come in.
I am rolling like a whale.
But I am a man.'
So went one of the songs, taught to some dreamer by the whale himself.
Indeed the whale was a "man," just as the salmon was.'[10]

The exalted harpooner now oversaw the butchering, and he first received the best meat from the back of the whale. This was treated ritually – and then given away. The rest of the meat was distributed according to rank and participation, while much of the blubber went to the assembled tribe. Choice portions of the fresh meat, tongue, lower jaw, flukes and flippers, were later eaten at a great feast thrown by the chief and his wife to honor the whale.

The blubber was particularly highly prized as it provided a significant amount of dietary oil. Oil of

Salmon – The Fish

various kinds, from other sea animals such as seal, walrus or enlackon,[11] was, together with that of the whale, an important staple in the diet of all the Northwest Coast tribes.[12] Various oils became important trade items together with dried fish, sturgeon, halibut, snapper and cod, from the Nootka to tribes in the south, such as the Salishan and Chinook, and was distributed to the interior groups via the great Dalles rendezvous on the Columbia River.

Less hazardous, but hardly less demanding in the skill and patience required, were the great salmon hunts of the Northwest Coast and Plateau people. In some Northwestern Indian languages, the word for 'fish' was simply the word for salmon. Salmon was **the** fish and, in fact, **the** food supply 'as important to the Indian as bread to the White'.[13] Although these large, powerful, deep-sea fish live in the sea for several years, they are actu-

This painted wooden totemic carving (above) is in the form of a salmon, the family totem of the Kuthouses of the Gun-ah-ho of the Tlingit. Salmon were far from the only fish in the Northwest but what made them distinct was the predictability of their cycle.

This masted boat (left) in use here with St Lawrence Island Eskimos is an *umiak*. Typically the sail was raised when it was being used for whale hunting. *Umiaks* were made of driftwood or a whale bone frame and covered with walrus or seal hides waterproofed with seal oil.

The Makah are famous for their whaling. This fishing line (above) is made of kelp and the floats of sealskin. Whaling required larger floats and a cedar-withe rope.

Two snowshoe-clad hunters (right) from the Subarctic stand next to their prey – two caribou from the great herds which roamed the continent every year, migrating from the forests to the tundra. For many tribes the caribou provided food and the raw materials to produce clothing, housing and utensils – the essentials of their life.

ally born in fresh water. During the summer months, a female salmon ready to lay her eggs, located the mouth of the river at the head of which, in the shallow waters, was her birthplace. She then commenced a journey upstream which could be up to 1,500 miles (2,414km), traveling perhaps four or five miles a day (8km) and never turning back. On meeting a rock, dam or waterfall, the salmon bent their 2-3ft (61-91cm) long bodies and leaped over them and 'Anyone who sets a trap or net with its mouth opening downstream can sometimes see it filled in a few minutes. Even when landed, salmon do not lie down and die, as weaker fish do. They jump like wildcats in the net and have to be clubbed to death'.[14]

Salmon formed a large part of the Plateau, as well as the Northwest Coast Indian diet; in season, they were baked, broiled or boiled. Immense quantities of salmon were also smoked or dried on scaffolds for trade and winter use. There was much ritual, ceremonial and myth associated with the fish. Widespread, for example, was the myth that no salmon really died and that the salmon were not fish at all but rather people who lived in a magic village under the sea.[15] The Bella Coola held a particular belief that twins were due to a salmon entering the body and it was said that for this reason, they had the power to induce the salmon runs by throwing gifts 'carved in red cedar wood as miniature salmon, into the river'.[16]

Buffalo, Moose and Caribou

Although the remains of an early species of buffalo, *Bison americanus*, have been found from Alaska to Georgia and traces have been discovered almost to the shores of the Atlantic coast, it was in the heartland of North America where it was concentrated in vast numbers and was a vital component in the life of the people who lived there – the Plains Indians.

While hunted in both winter and summer, the main hunts occurred in June, July and August when its flesh was in the best condition and the hair thin, enabling the pelts to be cleaned more easily on both sides. These skins were used for making *tipis*, shields, clothing, various bags, ropes and even boats. Other important buffalo products were sinew for sewing and bow strings, fiber for ropes, hair for ornament and some weaving, horns for spoons and drinking vessels and bone tools for hide-tanning and hoes. The horns were also worn as insignia of office,[17] while the dried droppings of the animal, often referred to as 'buffalo chips', were invaluable as a fuel.

A cow buffalo gave a yield averaging '400 pounds of meat produce';[18] much was cut into thin sheets, dried in the sun, made into pemmican, and packed away in parfleches for winter use. The marrow was also preserved in bladders and the tallow poured into skin bags.[19]

The immense dependence on the buffalo brought this animal in close touch with the people, it figured prominently in their religion, its habits gave designations to the months, it became a symbol of leadership and represented the good life and plenty. Myths and folk tales were replete in buffalo episodes, to the delight of young and old. Little wonder that the virtual extinction of this animal in the 1880s was the final death-knell of an ancient and rich culture of the tribes who lived within its range.

The most important large food animals in the Canadian Subarctic and vital to the economy of such tribes as the Chipewyan, Woods and West Main Cree, were the moose and caribou. The enormous moose, *Cervus alces*, unlike the buffalo

Given the importance of the caribou in the lives of many tribes, particularly the Chipewyan, it is no surprise that it featured prominently in the things they made and the motifs they used. This ivory carving (left) was made by an Inuit – note the legs which have been inserted separately. This serving dish (below) is decorated with three of the animals.

and caribou did not move in herds. Widely distributed throughout northern North America and
by nature solitary, one of its eating habits was
that of stripping the young bark and twigs of
trees. Moose were frequently hunted in the winter, being driven into deep snow to immobilize
them. The meat was lean and nutritious, the hide
used by both the Subarctic and Northeastern
tribes for clothing, was thick and heavy, while
moosehair embroidery – a technique of decoration
carried out by several tribes notably the Iroquois,
Huron and Ojibwa in these cultural areas – used
the fine hairs from the tail and bell of the moose.

Hunting the Caribou

The northern transitional forest and adjacent
tundra was the habitat of the so-called barren-
ground caribou, *Rangifer articus*, while to the
south and throughout the great boreal forests,
were the woodland caribou, *Rangifer caribou*,
moose, *Cervus alces*, and a few Woods buffalo, an
animal somewhat smaller than the Plains buffalo
further west.

The close relationship between the Indians of
this Subarctic region and the caribou, is exemplified by those bands of Chipewyan who occupied
the forest edges to the west of Hudson Bay,
referred to as *Ethen-eldèli*, 'caribou eaters' in the
Chipewyan language. Here, dependence
on the caribou and knowledge of
their migratory patterns, has
been likened to that
of the buffalo

hunters of the Great Plains, the Chipewyan material culture pattern being based on a complex of
products made from the hide, bone and antler of
the caribou. Thus, hides 'provided clothing, bedding, and lodge coverings, and also the babiche
(rawhide thong) used for bow strings, snowshoe
lacing, gill nets, tump-lines, drum-heads, and
other objects'.[20]

The method of hunting the caribou also resembled that of the 'pound' used by Plains Indians for
the buffalo and antelope, and like them was communal in nature. The caribou were driven into
the mouth of a chute made of poles or brush,
which led to a circular enclosure which could be
as much as a third of a mile in diameter. Unlike
the buffalo pound, however, snares were set and
the entangled caribou were dispatched with
spears and arrows. The meat from these great
kills was generally wind-dried, smoked in strips,
or pounded into powder for future use.

On occasions, the movements of the caribou
were erratic or unusual and in order to ensure a
kill, there was a complex communication network
between the scattered bands. So effective was this
interband organization that, as one distinguished
Subarctic anthropologist observed, 'Although in a
severe environment, the Chipewyan do not have
myths and legends which emphasize starvation'.[21]

The Eagle

Most bird species lent their plumage in the many
industries – clothing, war decorations, and ceremonial – of the North American Indian, but there

were some which were particularly sought. Paramount among these was the eagle, universally regarded as a majestic creature, its solitary nature and ability to soar high above earthbound man, endowed it with a mysterious and mystical nature, unsurpassed by any other creature.[22]

The mythology of most tribes makes repeated references to eagle beings and the widespread Thunderbird myths not infrequently relate the eagle to that awesome deity. Little wonder then that the feathers from this bird became coveted

items and that certain individuals specialized in hunting the eagle, its feathers being valuable trade items.

Not content, however, with the uncertainties of the hunt, the Pueblo tribes of the Southwest kept the eagle in captivity, with nearby shrines and associated winter ceremonials symbolically ensuring a continued abundance of eagles. The practice of keeping eagles and other birds in captivity was not exclusive to the Pueblo and was obviously ancient. Early reports, for example,

A symbol of power and liberty, the eagle was revered throughout North America. Possibly because of the height to which it frequently soared it was often considered to have communication with the Higher Powers and was often associated with the thunderbird of mythology. Eagle feathers were, and are still, highly prized and much used in ceremonial regalia such as this Sioux dance bustle (left) consisting of an eagle head and wings. It was said that a person holding an eagle feather told a lie at their peril.

Seeking to acquire supernatural power from an animal in a vision was a common enough aspect of an individual's life. For warriors the power derived from an eagle was among the most desirable. The eagle could strike swiftly, silently and with deadly accuracy – attributes any warrior yearned for. The warrior might invoke his spirit's assistance by using a personal ornament in conjunction with distinct paint schemes and a song; this particular object (below) is eagle talon medicine used by a Plains warrior.

relating to the Virginia Indians refer to the practice of keeping turkeys and eagles in cages for their feathers, while the Narraganset of the New England area kept tame hawks, not only for use of their plumage but also to frighten birds from the cultivated fields.[23]

Eagle Hunting

Soaring high, fast in flight, virtually inaccessible when at rest, the surest and most effective way of hunting an eagle was by use of concealed pits. Archeological evidence from the central and northern Plains, verifies the numerous traditions of the great antiquity of eagle-trapping which was practiced by most of the tribes who lived there and who used eagle feathers extensively on religious and ceremonial regalia. Among the most active of these tribes, who in turn traded them both east and west, were the Mandan and Hidatsa of the Missouri River region who developed lengthy rituals associated with the practice. As with all Mandan and Hidatsa ceremony, that of eagle catching had a mythological origin which told of two classes of small bears that had their concealed pits on the east and west bank of the Missouri. It was said that these mythological bears had seven eagle-trapping camps at which they were accustomed to meet in the autumn in order to catch young golden eagles.[24] Their expertise was brought to the Mandan tribe by a culture hero, Black Wolf,[25] who, befriended by black bears, was taught by them how to trap eagles.

Eagle catching was generally carried out in the autumn. The principal leaders owned special Eagle-trapping Medicine Bundles because of their interest in the mythology and rites associated with eagle-trapping, and were viewed as authorities on the subject, receiving 'popular recognition comparable to specialists in any other pursuit such as warfare or hunting'.[26] Expeditions were made up of volunteers and it was not unusual for wives and children to accompany the trappers, the whole expedition generally being viewed as something of an outing before the winter curtailed most outdoor activities.

When the leader acquired the Eagle-trapping Bundle, he also inherited associated hunting territory and on returning to the site each year, the first duty of the party was to repair the hunting lodge. Most hunting lodges, both in size and shape, resembled a *tipi*, but unlike the *tipi* a hide cover was not used – instead long poles were leaned together at the top to form a circular base and conical exterior. Large sheets of bark and earth were then banked around the outer lower edge of the lodge which was considered a sacred enclosure; towards the back was a buffalo-skull altar, flanked by snares, bird sticks, medicine bundles and sacred poles. These honored the snake spirits which could bring great hazard to the hunter when in the confined space of the eagle-trap pit. Concealed in a thicket of timber and located some distance from both the women's and children's camp and the eagle-trap itself, they ensured that the necessary stealth was achieved.[27]

Another essential feature was the sweat lodge, generally erected to the south of the trapping lodge. Here, purification of mind and body took place prior to the trapping.

The Eagle-trap

The eagle-trap consisted of a pit in the ground which was deep enough for the trapper to sit upright and since most were used annually, it was only necessary, each time, to clean out the pit which was then carefully covered with a matting of brush 'and it is said that grass and weeds were so cleverly interwoven with the brush and were placed above it in such a manner that a casual observer would not notice any difference between the trap and the hillside on which it was placed'.[28]

One Mandan informant who owned full eagle-trapping rights and who was considered an authority on eagle catching, always gave less experienced men some sound advice as to what they should do:

'When the eagle comes to the bait, it will be so close that you can see it through the grass covering over the pit. Use your right hand and catch the leg closest to you. Pull the bird down toward the ground, not toward you. Put out the left hand and get the other leg. Hold both legs with the left hand and put the right hand out and swing one wing over against the other. Hold both wings together at the tips, and the bird can't hurt you. Tie the feet together then. Eagles are strong and fierce. They can stick their claws through your hand, pick your face, or cut your face with their wings. Don't catch bald-headed eagles; they are fierce and will fight'.[29]

Two pendant groups of eagle feathers have been used to embellish this Plains coup stick (above), together with a smaller bunch of flicker feathers. The gaining of honor by touching the enemy with a coup stick (or by hand) was generally accorded higher status than killing him with a weapon.

This Kwakiutl grave effigy (right) depicts a chief with an eagle perched on his head to represent his clan figure. It was the Northwest Coast custom to mark graves with the deceased's totemic crest. Actual burial practices, however, did differ: the Tlingit and Tsimshian cremated; the Haida placed the body in the back of a pole or a box on top of it; while the Kwakiutl put the body in a box and placed it in a tree or cave.

Honoring the Eagle

On occasions, as the above suggests, the eagles were taken alive and might then be used as decoys. Most, however, were killed, either with a wood fiber snare or by breaking the bird's back. The value of the bird captured depended upon its age. Most prized was the so-called 'black tipped' bird, an immature golden eagle not yet four or five years of age whose tail feathers were the distinctive white with dark brown to black tips. Next, was the spotted golden eagle, while those from the bald-headed eagle were considered inferior.

As the hunters returned to base with the day's catch, the leaders commenced ceremonial crying; this continued right into the camp if a 'black tipped' bird had been caught.

Much ceremonial now took place. The birds were brought into the left side of the lodge while sage was burned as an incense for the objects used in the capture and songs were sung honoring the sacredness of the birds. A pipe was touched on the eagle's beak and white down feathers were removed from the Eagle Medicine Bundle to honor the eagle lodge and its contents. Such ceremonial was considered vital to the continued success of the hunters and it was always strictly observed. As one experienced eagle-trapper related, 'it was a very solemn thing to go out to catch eagles, and if a man were not serious he would not succeed'.[30]

The eagle-trapping expeditions could last up to two months, finally ending in a four day period of fasting and the closing of the Eagle-trapping Bundle. Then, members entered the sweat lodge, the leader chanting and talking to the eagle spirits:

'Eagles, go; leave us; go, everyone of you; . . .
Go to Birds Bill Butte; there you will find
antelope meat'.[31]

When the song ended, it was said that 'the spirits of the eagles left to join their people in the meeting place of the spirits near a large body of water'.[32] Then the leader sang a cleansing song,

and in carrying out this last act, he symbolically brought the men back to human beings, for when trapping it was considered that the men 'were impersonating the small bears',[33] who first taught the Mandans how to hunt eagles.

Intertribal Warfare – Trophies and Honors

Traditionally, individual or tribal ownership of land was a limited concept among the North American Indians but battles for choice hunting pastures, bounty, human captives, scalps, coups and glory were part of the tribal fabric.

Two kinds of intertribal warfare were generally recognized. One was defensive, fighting for the protection of the village, the other was aggressive, waged against the enemy and gaining honors which, particularly on the Plains, were achieved by a complex 'coup' counting system.

The stone-headed club (far left) and pipe tomahawk (near left) are two of the most common types of Indian weapon. The Northern Cheyenne sandstone-headed club, with beaded handle, is of an older style, wholly indigenous and was often carried by warriors on foot. This Sioux tomahawk – a combination of weapon and pipe – dates from the post-contact trade-acquisition period.

War parties – or more frequently raiding parties assembled for the purpose of capturing horses – often included boys in their number. Boys were raised in the belief that it could be honorable, to die young in battle. Aspiring youngsters emulated the examples offered by their tribe's great warriors who generally acted prudently on the battlefield. These Arapaho youths (left) are old enough to have seen their share of action, but by the time this photograph was taken in the 1870s the warrior's way of life was largely at an end on the southern Plains.

Possibly the most notable warrior band of the Lakota was the Oglala, the band of Red Cloud, Crazy Horse and Gall. He Dog (right) or *Sunka Bloka* was an Oglala warrior, distinguished tribal historian and friend of Crazy Horse in whose camp he was a sub-chief. In 1930 he was the last surviving representative of the Oglala grand councillors – chiefs of the highest rank and referred to as the *wicasa yatapika*, or supreme head men.

The knife was a favored weapon of Northwest Coast warriors who preferred something for use at close-range when launching early morning surprise attacks on their enemies. This double-edged steel-bladed Tlingit dagger (right) has a handle inlaid with shell and carved in the form of a clan bear. In use, the strap was wrapped around the wrist to prevent the knife being dropped. Interclan grievances among the Tlingit were settled by formal combat between clan champions, hence the use of clan symbols as decor.

The aim of such warfare, however, was seldom to annihilate the enemy. Thus, with revenge satisfied, the spoils became paramount – horses, slaves, women, children, and particularly in the case of the Iroquois, a brave adversary to put to death by ritual torture.

The Scalp

Anciently, and throughout most of North America, an important trophy of war was the head of the enemy, although arms and leg portions were not uncommonly taken by the tribes of the Southeast. On the Plains, some Cheyenne warriors took the fingers and even, on occasions, the testicles of their fallen foe. The scalp, however, was a very convenient way of designating triumph over an enemy. It could be easily removed, was light-weight, could be preserved and, when embellished, was decoratively attached to costume or war regalia for all to see.[34]

who lived through the ordeal, with a peculiar popping similar to 'the noise of bubbles or blisters popping'.[38]

The practice of scalping was rapidly spread by the encouragement in the form of scalp bounties offered by the colonial governments. Thus, for example, in the 1650s, the Dutch in New York – and later the English and French – offered high payment for those scalps taken from hostile Indians in the region. This European slant on an ancient custom was, as we shall see, a far cry from the original concepts associated with the scalp, human hair having much symbolic and religious significance and the ritual of the Scalp Dance was an important ceremonial in the cultural areas where scalping was practiced.

The Raid for Slaves

Among most of the Northwest Coast tribes – although head-hunting was sometimes practiced – war expeditions were almost solely undertaken for the purpose of capturing people for slaves. The Klamath word for slave is *lugsh* which translates as 'to carry a load', emphasizing that slaves were viewed as the 'carriers of the tribe'.[39] So deeply embedded was the concept of slavery among the Northwest Coast tribes – such as the Tlingit, Haida, Chinook, Makah and Klamath – that much of their economy and social organization, which gave great weight to wealth as status, pivoted on the number of slaves an individual owned.[40] The fabulous wealth of a Tlingit chief was sometimes demonstrated in the rit-

Medicine Pipe (left), or *Lahaktanduheshaadu*, a chief of the Grand Pawnee photographed in about 1865. His magnificent bear claw necklace was typical attire for a warrior of status. The Pawnee were closely allied to the Omaha with whom they fought against the Sioux and Cheyenne.

The operation of scalping, although painful, was by no means fatal and it is well recorded that several individuals who had been scalped, lived to tell the tale.[35] Young warriors, it seems, were sometimes affected by the bloody process. Thus the scout, Le Forge, reported that several times he noted his Crow companions acting strangely; when they took a scalp, they appeared decidedly nervous and on two occasions he saw a warrior pause during the operation in order to vomit.[36]

The portion taken was usually a circular patch of skin at the base of the scalplock just below the crown of the head.[37] The scalplock itself was a small braid of hair hanging from the back of the head. In the regions where the custom of scalping was particularly well-established in the Historic Period, such as the Northeast and Plains, it was generally decorated with quillwork, beads or feathers. The operation was comparatively easy to perform and it came away, according to one

These Pima mesquite wood war clubs (above) differ from those of the Woodlands or Plains but are similar to the jaw-breaking clubs developed by the Yuman tribes.

This Nootka war club (right) is distinctively Northwest in form. Made of wood, shell, stone and hair, variants of this type of club were often called 'slave killers', although little evidence exists that they had that function.

US Army commanders with experience of the campaigns on the Plains and in the Southwest believed that the Apache (below) were the finest Indian warriors of all. In fact, a comparison is not really possible since their approaches to warfare were very different. What is true is that just a few could tie down far greater numbers of troops.

ual killing of slaves at the time of erection of his plank house. Less brutal was the giving away, sometimes freeing, of slaves during the great winter ceremonials of the Northwest Coast tribes – the potlatch – thereby demonstrating that the owner was so wealthy he could easily afford to part with such valuable property.

Armored Warriors

When fully equipped for war, a 19th century Tlingit warrior was armed with a special fighting knife and, additionally, he would probably carry a war club, short spear and bow and arrows.

The warrior wore a heavy moosehide sleeveless tunic over which was an armor-like covering made of wooden rods and slats, the whole extending from the neck to the knees. On his head and neck were a helmet and wooden collar, the helmet carved with animal crests or ferocious human faces to strike fear into the enemy. At other times, however, as reported by Laguna, 'for greater

mobility, the warrior might pin his hair on top of his head (like a shaman) and wear only a hide tunic, both face and shirt painted with his clan crests'.[41]

Body armor was not exclusive to the Northwest Coast tribes; indeed, there is considerable evidence which suggests that multilayered hide armor had virtually intercontinental distribution[42] and descriptions by Lewis and Clark of Shoshoni armor, which they observed in use in 1804, are remarkably close to those of the multilayered body armor worn by Patagonians in southern South America.[43] The Sioux symbolically retained the armor in the single layered skin 'war shirt' which, in the Historic Period, could only be worn by men of military distinction.[44]

The War-Club and Tomahawk

Although, as in most cultural areas, the bow was used from an early period by the tribes of

Although it existed in many places, protective body armor was particularly well developed along the western seaboard. This rod and slat armor , bound with sinew and rawhide, was collected from the Tlingit in the 1880s. The central slat panel was often embellished with a symbolic clan crest in red and black paint.

An irony of the closing military campaigns against the Indians was the pronounced use of scouts familiar with the terrain and methods of their opponents. That many were recruited from traditional enemies – the Pawnee and Crow who fought against the Sioux, for example – is not surprising; more poignant is the knowledge that a few took up arms against their own people, such as these Modoc and Klamath scouts (left) who in 1872 helped to subdue a more independent portion of the tribe led by *Kintpuash*.

the Northeast[45], a much-favored weapon in native warfare was the wooden ball-headed club, made from ironwood and up to 2ft (61cm) in length. By the early 1700s, such weapons were progressively falling into disuse for warfare, but they were retained for ceremonial purposes and were even to be found among the tribes of the central Plains, such as the Sioux and Crow, well into the 19th century.

This traditional weapon was replaced by the trade tomahawk, the most ingenious of which combined a weapon with a pipe – hence the term, 'pipe tomahawk'. These were sometimes thrown in battle, one 1770 traveler reporting that in pur-

suing an enemy, 'the Indians threw their tomahawks with the utmost dexterity and seldom failed "striking it into the skull or back of those they pursue" . . . '[46] Such skill in handling a tomahawk was greatly admired and displayed: thus, the scholar, Lewis Henry Morgan, in describing an Iroquois war council, tells of the assembled warriors approving the speeches by throwing their tomahawks high into the air and estimating the end-over-end turning of the weapon so accurately that they caught them by the hafts as they came down.[47]

The Demise of the Huron

At almost continuous war with the Iroquois, in particular the Seneca, the Huron's ancient style of combat was dramatically changed as the effects of Euroamerican culture reverberated through the Woodlands of the Northeast and impacted on distant Huronia. First, steel-tipped arrowheads and spears, metal tomahawks and then the gun, progressively rendered Huron armor – which formerly made them such formidable opponents – virtually useless. The effects were partially offset by the Huron's trade with the French for furs in return for European goods which included guns. But the respite was short lived; Dutch, and later English, pacts with the Iroquois led to a concerted effort on the part of that powerful confederation to eliminate all opposition in the lucrative fur trade.[48] Thus, by the middle of the 17th century, both the aims as well as the nature of warfare between traditional enemies, changed. Now, combined forces of Seneca, Onondaga, Cayuga and, on occasions, Oneida, continuously raided and destroyed the villages of the Huron tribes,[49] who were already weakened by a series of smallpox and other epidemics. The destruction was systematic and well-coordinated, the Mohawks – the most easterly of the Iroquois confederation –

Ball-headed war clubs were much favored by the Northeast Woodlands tribes whose warriors were extremely skilled in their use, even throwing them with deadly accuracy in order to strike a foe at a distance. This particular club (above) is actually Yankton Sioux. It dates from the 1870s, and bears testimony to the widespread and continued use of such styles.

American Horse (right), or *Wasechua-tasunka*, was the son-in-law of Red Cloud with whom he traveled to Washington on several occasions, during one of which this photograph was taken in 1877. A great orator, he was well versed in treaty complexities.

blocking all trade routes to the St. Lawrence waterway; as Heidenreich observed:

'In 1648 the large village of Teanaustaye and a neighboring one were destroyed and Saint Ignace abandoned . . . by mid-1649 all villages east of Sainte Marie were abandoned . . . [and] in a grand council with the Jesuits the Huron then made the decision to abandon Huronia'.[50]

From an estimated population in the early-17th century of some 20,000 people, the numbers plummeted and the Huron as an organized tribe all but ceased to exist. By 1905, fewer than 1,000 laid claim to a Huron heritage. It was a pattern which would be repeated many times as the Euroamerican culture spread westwards, changing the life of the Indian forever.

The canoe was a central element of Northwest Coast life and, inevitably, it featured in the region's warfare – even if only in the form of transport to enable slave raids to be undertaken. Sometimes sharpened paddles were used in case of a direct canoe-to-canoe action.

A symbolic image of a way of life fast disappearing. For lone warriors such as this Shoshoni man (left) along the trail in Wyoming Territory in 1859, the horse remained but the range was curtailed and the raiding and warfare were a memory to be rekindled only in stories around the campfire.

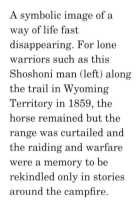

RELIGION, CEREMONIAL AND CHANGE

> *'Religious ceremonies express a tribe's attempts to order its spiritual and physical world through the power of the word, whether chanted, spoken or sung. Ceremonies, and the songs, narratives and orations included in them, may be expressed in special forms of language.'*
>
> LA VONNE BROWN RUOFF[1]

A S WITH MOST PEOPLES, the belief in the existence of higher powers was very strong in the mind of the American Indian, the concepts being progressively modified with increased contact with the Euroamerican. Recent studies, however, have challenged the view that the white race alone possessed a knowledge of God. The Omaha scholar, Francis La Flesche, for example, who studied the religion of his and related people, the Osage, was in a position to compare the religious concepts of both races, and found that there were acute linguistic difficulties and that both form and spirit of American Indian thinking were frequently lost in the literal translations by white scholars. Such translations were often used to judge the mental capacity of the Indian and to draw conclusions about his concept of the 'Supreme Being' and led to gross distortion in the conclusions regarding Native American religion.[2]

Powers of the Universe

Religious concepts centered around a deep desire to obtain, and retain, the good will of the friendly spiritual powers and also to control those which were hostile. A widely held view of the spiritual world perhaps most strongly developed by Algonquian speaking tribes of the Woodlands and the Great Plains[3] identified a cosmology which recognized a universe consisting of three parallel worlds and which, fundamentally, were not much different from the Christian's ideas of hell, earth and heaven. There were the underwater spirits in the lake on which the earth floated and spirits in the animals and plants both on land and in the water. Then, above the earth, beyond the dome of the blue sky, lay the realm of the upper world, dominated by spirits matching those of the underworld.[4] Among the most powerful of these were the Thunderbirds who, by flashing their eyes and flapping their wings, produced lightning and thunder.

As with Christianity and many other religions where the concept of God incorporates several deities, often evoking the sacred number three, so too with North American Indians. This is well illustrated by the religious concepts of the Lakota – the Plains Sioux – which have been subjected to considerable analysis. Here, the number four, a sacred number in many North American cultural areas, predominates. In the Lakota *Tobtob Kin* or 'Four-times-four', a hierarchy of spirits totaling 16 are clearly defined and linked by the shamans. More complex then than the Father, Son, and Holy Ghost whom Christians refer to as God.[5]

The similarity between the religious concepts and actions of the Sioux and those of the missionaries who were trying so hard to convert them was recognized by at least one literate 19th century Plains warrior, Left Handed, who observed, 'The Catholics are strange; their religion is like the old Dakota religion. The priest has water in his rattle; our medicine men use beads or stones. They mumble something called Latin. Medicine men mumble and yell'.[6]

Above all else there was a unity to the world view exhibited in all Indian cultures: ceremonial, religion, human behavior, the natural world – all were subject to mysterious connections and influences. This affected daily life, art and culture (the flora depicted in this Woodlands embroidery, right and far left, reflect the native respect for it), and so on – it had a far-reaching effect on most things. Dances could be social or ceremonial – invariably they were both. These Apache *Gahan* Dancers or Mountain Spirits (main picture) represent a central feature of the Apache belief system and they remain so today. Native religions reached a low point with the Ghost Dance era in the late-19th century; defeated and forced to adapt to a new way of life being imposed on them, many turned to it in desperation and paid with their lives - this wand (above left) dates from that grim time.

107

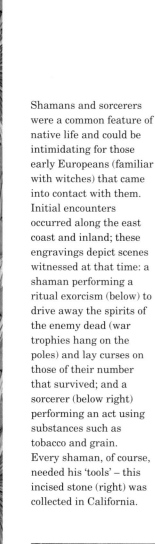

Shamans and sorcerers were a common feature of native life and could be intimidating for those early Europeans (familiar with witches) that came into contact with them. Initial encounters occurred along the east coast and inland; these engravings depict scenes witnessed at that time: a shaman performing a ritual exorcism (below) to drive away the spirits of the enemy dead (war trophies hang on the poles) and lay curses on those of their number that survived; and a sorcerer (below right) performing an act using substances such as tobacco and grain. Every shaman, of course, needed his 'tools' – this incised stone (right) was collected in California.

The Soul

In addition, there were almost universally, lines of thought which led to the belief in a soul, separate from the body, frequently in human form and continuing to exist after death. One was the formation of the concept of the 'power of acting' which, although resident in the body, was distinct from the existence of the body.[7]

This lack of tangibility of the soul led to a widespread belief that it could only be seen by the shamans – although it was conceded that the common man did, on occasions, obtain a fleeting glimpse of it. To the Algonquians, it was but a transient shadow, while the Shasta claimed that only the trail or footprints of a soul could be seen which remained nearby for five days after the death of a person and then traveled to the Milky Way.[8]

Widespread was the identification of the soul with the owl, its flitting motions and human likeness combining and leading to the idea of an intangible soul of a dead person and a powerful belief in the existence of the soul after death. Thus, the Algonquian of the Northeast Woodlands said that the souls of the deceased resided in the west with the brother of their great culture hero.[9]

Belief in visits to the world of the dead by people who have been in a trance or on a spirit quest was commonly-held, leading to widespread acceptance of the teachings of the Paiute dreamer and medicine man, Wovoka, who while in a feverish trance claimed to have gone to the spirit world and to have been instructed by God. The outcome was the Spirit or Ghost Dance which swept the Great Basin, Plateau and Plains in the late 1880s and led to the tragedy of Wounded Knee in December 1890.

Enslaved Souls

As was discussed in the previous chapter, the practice of scalping was ancient. According to Father Le Petit (1730), the Natchez and all the other 'Nations of Louisiana' bestowed names upon warriors according to their conduct in battle, the venerable war chiefs distributing these names 'according to the merit of the warriors'. To deserve the title of great man-slayer, 'it is necessary to have taken 10 slaves or to have carried off 20 scalps'.[10] The taking of the scalp was a particularly serious affair with a strict penance imposed: they 'do not sleep at their return with their wives, and do not eat any meat . . . this abstinence lasts for six months' and failing to observe it 'they imagine that the soul of him whom they have killed will cause them to die through sorcery, that they will never again obtain any advantage over their enemies, and that the slightest wounds they may receive will prove fatal'.[11] In these regions, scalps represented those of the enemy whose souls would be slaves to the slayer in the next world; symbolically, scalping then was an insurance of the good life hereafter, and captured the soul of the warrior who, alive, would be more than useless.[12]

Similar concepts were also held in pre-horse days by the Plains Indians. Thus, on the return of a successful Piegan war party (circa 1725), the conclusion was that 'those who had taken the trophy from the head of an enemy who they had killed, said the Souls . . . belong to us and we have given them to our relations in the other world to be their slaves, and we are contented'.[13]

A century or more later, the Blackfeet still continued to put high value on the scalp as a war trophy, and thus it was 'ahead of the capture of a horse from the enemy'.[14] However, European technology was having an influence on Plains warfare for at this time it ranked lower than the capture of an enemy's gun.[15] Nevertheless, human hair was still considered to have potency and when worn on garments it endowed the wearer with power.[16] In the Southwest, for example, it has been reported that great emphasis was put on removing from the slayer the 'dangerous supernatural potency of the scalp'.[17]

The Origin of Disease

Universally, disease was regarded as a mysterious force often due to the evil influence of animal or other spirits, and herbs and roots were used for medicinal purposes.

The association of disease and animal spirits is well-illustrated by the Cherokee account of the origin of disease and medicine which relates that in ancient days quadrupeds, birds, fishes and insects could all talk and they and the human race lived together in peace and friendship. Unfortunately, as time passed, the number of human beings increased so rapidly that the animals began to find themselves cramped for room. The problem was further compounded by the fact that man also invented weapons and

On the Northwest Coast a curing shaman's most important item was the soul catcher. This Tlingit example (above) is made from bone and inlaid with abalone shell. Illness could be diagnosed as a result of the soul having left the body and it therefore had to be enticed back in order to effect a cure.

The tribes of the Southeast used purgative drinks to cleanse the body by inducing vomiting (above). The best known such ritual is the Black Drink found among the Cherokee, Choctaw, Creek and Seminole.

began killing the animals for their flesh and skins and so the animals resolved to council upon the measures to be taken for their common safety.

Some decided to protect themselves by introducing various diseases – the deer inflicted rheumatism, the fish and reptiles, loss of appetite. Thus, the animals devised and named the multitude of diseases which inflict mankind.

The Use of Herbs

When the plants, who were friendly to mankind, heard what the animals had done, they determined to defeat their evil designs:

'Each tree, shrub, and herb, down even to the grasses and mosses, agreed to furnish a remedy for some one of the diseases named, and each said: "I shall appear to help man when he calls upon me in his need". Thus did medicine originate, and the plants, every one of which has its use if we only knew it, furnish the antidote to counteract the evil wrought by the revengeful animals. When the doctor is in doubt what treatment to apply for the relief of a patient, the spirit of the plant suggests to him the proper remedy'.[18]

Herbs, however, were not just used in the treatment of disease but were also employed for the purpose of healing wounds – and the success was often dramatic. Almost without exception, medical aid was given with considerable ceremony usually with drums, rattle and song. Some ceremonials, as among the Navajo, were very elaborate – and costly.

Not all animals were at war with mankind, however, the buffalo generally being viewed as a great spiritual benefactor.

How the Buffalo Society Treated Wounds

To the Omaha Buffalo Society was committed the knowledge of medicines to cure wounds. The Society consisted of individuals to whom the buffalo spirits had appeared in dreams and given instructions for curing. Various roots were used for healing, portions being ground between the teeth and then water was taken into the mouth, and the medicated liquid was 'blown with force into the wound'.[19] The Omaha scholar, Francis La Flesche, recorded the effectiveness of the treatment carried out by members of the Buffalo Society when he witnessed the accidental shooting of a boy by a young man. The boy had been badly wounded; the women were wailing and many thought that he was dead. Then, a tall man wrapped in a buffalo robe appeared:

'He stooped over the child, felt his wrist, and then his heart. "He is alive," the man said; "set up a tent and take him in". The little body was lifted on a robe and carried by two men into a large tent that had been hastily erected. Meanwhile a young man had been sent in all haste to call the buffalo doctors. Soon they were seen galloping over the hill on their horses, one or two at a time, their long hair flowing over their naked backs'.[20]

The curing ceremonials now commenced and there was a clear distinction between two types of physicians who differed in their influence over the patient. The Sioux referred to such individuals as *wakan witshasha*, 'mystery man' and the other as *pejihuta witshasha* 'grass root man'.[21]

Some 20 or more buffalo men now sat around the boy and one of their number told how the buffalo had, in a vision, revealed to him the secret of the medicine he used and the song which went with it. The root medicine was now prepared and putting the pieces of root into his mouth together with a mouthful of water, 'he approached the boy bellowing and pawing the earth like an angry buffalo at bay. When near the boy he drew in a long breath, and with a whizzing noise forced the water from his mouth into the wound'. Throughout the proceedings the assembled Buffalo Society members, which included two women, sang 'with a volume that could be heard a mile away'. The treatment lasted four days, although on the third day the buffalo doctors pro-

nounced the boy out of danger. Then the doctors sang the song of triumph and the fees were now distributed – horses, robes, bear-claw necklaces, eagle feathers and embroidered leggings. Within a month or so, La Flesche recorded the boy 'was back among us, ready to play or to watch another pistol practice by the young men'.[22]

Altars and Shrines

An important feature in the performance of many Native American ceremonials was the use of an altar, some of which were relatively simple. The Blackfeet, for example, used a 'smudge altar' for almost every formal religious ceremonial, sweetgrass (*Sevastana odorata*) usually being dropped onto a glowing ember at the center of an altar made from colored earths. Similar colored earth altars were used in the Southwest and as Wissler

The buffalo as a ceremonial animal was not restricted to the Plains, it featured in the Southwest too. These dancers (below left) from Tesuque pueblo were photographed in 1925 and would have been accompanied in their dance by Buffalo Girl.

Rattles identical to this (below) were used in the four-day *O-kee-pa* Ceremony of the Mandan that featured the Buffalo Bull Society performing a dramatic variant of the Buffalo Calling Dance.

These Sioux men (right) are preparing for their *inikagapi*, or 'taking a sweat'. The traditional sweat lodge is made from bent saplings covered with animal hides. Warriors took sweat baths as ritual purificaton prior to battle, but they were also undertaken for relaxation and cleanliness. The steam came from heated stones over which water was poured. The heat and perspiration caused a feeling of transformation. The warm, dark, cramped interior might be seen as a womb from which one emerged born anew.

The Flute Ceremony was a rainmaking ritual and one of the most important of Hopi ceremonial events. It was held in late August on alternate years with the Snake Dance and took 16 days. Prior to the public aspect there were several secretive days spent in the *kiva* singing and praying before a sand altar. This photograph (right) was taken at a sacred spring at Third Mesa in 1900. The procession then proceeded to the village, taking with it three pottery jars containing water and fetishes.

observed, such arrangements were 'continuous throughout a large section of the continent'.[23]

Altars in the Southwest, such as those of the various Pueblos – Hopi and Zuni for example – and of the Navajo, were often complex affairs. The Pueblo Flute Ceremony used an altar with associated feeding bowls, carrying baskets, rattles, pipes and prayer sticks together with various styles of dry-painting which made reference to the cardinal points.[24] The ceremonials associated with the construction of such altars date back to very ancient times. So too with the fetish which was most highly developed by the Zuni who had the reputation for being most skillful in their production and had religious associations which extended back eons.[25]

Fetishes and Tutelars

As with the Cree Indians of the northern Plains who were a traditional source of certain types of personal medicine bundles such that 'Cree medicine' gained the reputation of having great power,[26] so the Zuni were viewed in the Southwest as a source for tutelar type charm by members of other tribes. For example, the Navajo sought special pieces of banded calcite for use as prayer sticks; to the Zuni, however, many of these were actually considered to be fetishes which reflected the religious intellectual core of their culture. The Zuni considered that the sun, moon, stars, the sky, earth, and sea, 'in all their phenomena and elements', and all inanimate objects, as well as plants, animals and men, belonged to one great system of all-conscious and interrelated life 'in which the degrees of relationship seem to be determined largely, if not wholly, by the degrees of resemblance'.[27] Among the most valued fetishes were those natural concretions or objects which had a resemblance to animals even though this similarity was often heightened by artificial means. Others, however, were more complex and moved well beyond the realm of personal charms, such as *Ettone*, a fetish of the Rain Priests, which symbolized 'Mother Earth, rain and all of the life-giving forces upon which man depends'.[28]

Clear and away from the fetish was the 'totem'[29] or personal tutelary which was seldom, if ever, parted with by its owner. A totem was symbolic of the patron or guardian spirit, a concept widely recognized among the Indians where most persons acquired them during puberty ceremonials. Even with some of the less organized but linguistically related groups such as those in California the acquisition of a guardian spirit at the age of puberty was a vital feature of their religious beliefs, the totem being obtained through definitely prescribed rituals.[30] Generally, the totem was some animal or bird but it could be a translucent or black stone, a tuft of hair, feathers, even a small shell. Unlike the fetish, the personal totem was not an object of worship but rather something which connected its owner with the higher powers which it represented and it was not unusual for those individuals who had similar totems to join a religious or cult society.[31]

Thus, among the Omaha, those members of the Buffalo Society, referred to earlier, had gained entrance by virtue of a dream of a buffalo while Bear Society members had seen a bear during the ritual of their vision.[32] A requirement of the Omaha tutelary complex was to seek out the bird or animal seen, kill it and then select some small part to keep on his person. Such a custom would, however, have been abhorrent to the Iroquois who regarded their own destiny and life spans as closely connected to the totem animal. Pictographs of such totem animals were used to signify Iroquois clan membership – turtle, wolf, bear, beaver, deer, snipe, hawk etc.,[33] and during their Midwinter ceremony[34] representations of the totem were made of wood, bone, antler or some other material and given to the youth to keep and carefully preserve as a symbol of his or her guardian power.

Ceremonial and Ritual

Basic to much of American Indian thinking was a recognition of mankind's oneness with the uni-

Powerful and elaborate masks were used in many parts of the Arctic and Subarctic regions. Both these examples are Yup'ik. This spectacular one (above) is from the area around the lower Kuskokwim River, its X-ray style for the spirit figure astride an animal, possibly a beaver, being characteristic of the Yup'ik. The dancing mask (below) is similarly replete with composite imagery to reflect the multiplicity of souls believed to inhabit each spirit being. A spirit had to be accorded respect because of its ability to bestow benificence or malice to humans.

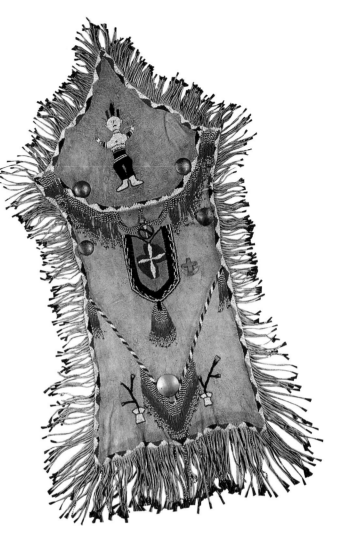

This Apache buckskin dance apron (right) is embellished with German silver discs, tin cone tinklers and glass beads. Its purpose is unknown, but it may have been used in one of the most famous of Apache ceremonials, a young woman's coming of age when elaborate regalia was worn.

This 16th century engraving of a Southeastern ceremony is thought to depict a fertility dance – possibly related to the famous Green Corn Dance – at which the Higher Powers were honored in return for an abundant harvest.

verse and the absolute necessity of maintaining this harmony through ritual and ceremonial.

The style of ceremonial and associated rituals differed markedly even within a cultural area; for example, the Pawnee 'Spring Awakening' ceremonials[35] put great emphasis on song while the Mandan *O-kee-pa* emphasis was on fantastical dance. A pattern paralleled in the Southwest with the Navajo subdued curing ceremonies and associated sand paintings which contrast with the lengthy dramas of the Hopi Powamu Kachina[36] or Apache Mountain Spirit Dancers.[37] Others, such as the spectacular Sun Dance, which was performed by many Plains tribes, involved a combination of prayer, contemplation, dance and drama, some private but much public. Although there were considerable variations, a common thread was one of renewal, revitalizing and replenishing the resources of nature.[38]

In addition to the tribal ceremonials there were many which were connected with the numerous cult societies, which were not infrequently

embedded in historical past events and often enhanced by myth and legend. Thus, in ancient times, the Zuni were said to have had a great battle with the Apache, an intrusive and warlike Athapascan tribe who migrated from the far north in the 14th century and this event seems to have been integrated into a War God cult. Wooden war god effigies commemorating this and other events were traditionally set up to guard the entrance to tribal shrines on the hilltops near the Zuni villages.[39]

Healing Ceremonials

The lengthy curing rites associated with the Southwest and mentioned earlier, were not exclusive to this cultural area for among the most important of the cult societies in the Northeast were those associated with healing, the Chippewa *Midewiwin* putting emphasis on the prolonging of life by 'right living'.[40] The records and teachings of the *Midewiwin* were inscribed with a bone stylus on birch bark rolls, their complex significance

These Zuni War God effigies (left) were placed as guards at the entrance to a tribal shrine on Twin Mountain. Traditionally such effigies had to be carved from trees struck by lightning. They were particularly important deities during the time when the Zuni had active warrior societies because of their frequent conflicts with the Apache. The warrior societies venerated *Ahayuta*, their elder god of war. The war gods symbolism still figures in annual ceremonies.

being taught to initiates. Every member of the society possessed a special bag made of the skin of a bird or animal in which were contained the medicinal herbs and charms which the person had been taught to use. These bags were viewed as having great power and in the *Mide* songs they were sometimes represented as speaking. For example, one initiation song contained the words, 'There comes a sound from my medicine bag,' and another relating to an owlskin medicine bag, 'I am the one who is trying to fly. He is making it (the medicine)'.[41] The employment of these special bags for healing was derived from a tradition connected with the origin of the society,

'four *Mide* manido [spirits] with the colors of the dawn painted on their foreheads came out of the eastern sky, each carrying a live otter in his hand. They used these otters as the *Mide* bags are now used in ceremonies of the society, and by this means they restored to life a young man who had been dead eight

days. They instructed the Indians to continue this custom'.[42]

The *Mide* sacred bag was replaced to the north and east by masks as symbols of spirit forces which both Iroquoian and Algonquian tribes contended had a marked influence on their welfare. Nowhere was this more emphasized than in the so-called False Face Society of the Iroquois. The masks were not for the purpose of concealment but rather acted as a symbol which operated on the principle of 'substituting a part for the whole, and the wearer behaves as if he were the supernatural being whom he impersonates'.[43] The supernatural spirits of the Wind or Disease Gods were considered to be of two classes and several varieties being portrayed by carved wooden or braided (sometimes woven) faces that figured in the myths.[44]

According to ancient Iroquois traditions, a strange creature which had an enormous head with flaring eyes made his home on a huge rock

115

over which his hair streamed like water. The spirits with ugly visages that had the power to inflict ailments and send disease among people, were also associated with the Wind Spirit and it was these traditional mythological figures 'that suggested the use of the falseface masks'.[45] Traditionally, it was said that the preliminary carving of a False Face mask was done on a living tree with much associated ceremonial which might extend over three days, offerings of tobacco being made, all to ensure that the healing potency of the tree was kept within the mask. 'Sacred tobacco was burned, a pinch at a time, as a plea for forgiveness to the Tree Spirit for the necessity of mutilating the tree. The tobacco smoke was blown into the roots and among the branches. Because of this offering of tobacco, it was thought the tree would not die, and the scars left on the tree would heal over in from two or four years'.[46] The powers of the finished mask also demanded special treatment; tobacco had to be burned for them periodically and 'they should not be closed up in boxes'.[47]

The False Face curing ceremonials were generally held in January or February of each year. A typical curing ritual was carried out by the masked man first dipping his hands into hot ashes and laying them onto the patient; he then blew through cupped hands at the same time rubbing them over the ill person.[48] Few doubted that if good will of the supernatural beings had been achieved – by appropriate ritual and feasting – a miraculous cure would follow.

Destruction and Change

Long before the white man reached North America, the appearance and disappearance of fur-bearing animals and their movement from one part of the country to another, had an immense influence on the lifestyle and location of the Indian tribes. For example, in the 16th century, the Plains Apache were trading buffalo hides to the Pecos who, acting as middlemen, bartered them again with the Zuni. Such extensive trade was common in the region long 'before the advent of the Europeans'.[49]

The early-1600s saw a sudden extension of this ancient trade as the French looked to their Canadian possessions. The region abounded in beaver and the underfur of this creature was the best material available for the production of the felt required for manufacturing the highly fashionable broad-brimmed Swedish hat, and the demand for luxury furs, which extended to otter, fox, raccoon, marten and lynx, progressively increased.

The effect on the economy of the various tribes was profound, the goods now being offered by white traders stimulating an expansion in the trapping of fur-bearing animals.[50] It also increased conflict between tribes as the balance of power was shifted and tribal territories expanded to meet the new demand.

As the fur trade extended progressively west and indigenous creatures were all but exterminated, the lifestyle of the Indian was changed forever. Thus, on the Great Plains both economy and ceremonial were dramatically affected with the disappearance of the buffalo in the 1880s and less than a score of years later the impact of the fur trade in the Subarctic region 'very much altered the character of the northern Indians'.[51]

The spiritual as well as the economic base of the Indian was also progressively eroded. A widespread attitude which prevailed in various forms in a 200 year (or more) period, was summed up by that of the French authorities who 'insisted that Jesuit missionaries be tolerated among the tribes as a condition of continued trade'.[52]

In his detailed studies of Osage religious beliefs and practices, the Omaha Indian and anthropologist, Francis La Flesche, was led to the widespread conclusion that a people's mental capacity and intellectual achievements found their greatest expression in religion.[53] Such achievements, however, were not recognized by the many missionaries who, in increasing numbers and starting in the early 1600s, attempted to convert the American Indian to Christianity and so change the very foundations of their culture forever.

The Jesuits and the Huron

By 1629, a number of Roman Catholic missionaries had visited the Huron and within a decade or so the Jesuit Fathers succeeded in establishing a virtual monopoly of mission work in New France, converting more than 100 Hurons each year, impressing them with such knowledge as the 'ability to predict eclipses'.[54]

The Hurons, the Jesuits obviously hoped, 'could be duped into thinking that the Jesuits possessed

A Grand Medicine Dance photographed (left) at Lac Courte Oreille Reservation, Wisconsin, in 1899. This was one of the most important ceremonies of the Chippewa *Midewiwin*. Note the child and its mother within the framework lodge with an offering of blankets.

This Iroquois mask was a powerful element in the ceremonies of the False Face Society undertaken in order to appease the spirits and effect a cure for all sorts of ailments. The face is distorted to represent the disease spirit whose face was damaged when the Iroquois' Creator caused him to smash his face into a mountain. In awe of the Creator's power the spirit offered his services to the Iroquois in return for a promise to honor him in their rituals.

Because of their leading role in the fur trade the Huron were more exposed than many other tribes to the French and their missionaries or 'Black Robes'. The Huron blamed the latter and their religion for the epidemics which ravaged the tribe and reduced its population by half between 1635 and 1641. Shown here (above) is Father Hennepin, a French Franciscan friar who accompanied the French explorer Rene Robert Cavelier, Sieur de La Salle, when they became possibly the first white men to see the Niagara Falls.

supernatural powers'.[55] The effect, however, was only partial, relatively few Hurons actually being influenced by these methods alone; conversions were, in fact, for more practical reasons. Thus, converted Hurons were given the status of privileged customers when they traded with the French and received higher prices for their furs than the non-Christian Hurons and after 1641 they were allowed more readily to purchase muskets. Although such realities led to the baptism of many Hurons, it also caused great stress within the daily life of the tribe, missionaries insisting, for example, that the converts should not attend any traditional Huron ceremonials and rituals.[56]

Within a few years, Huron intellectuals increasingly recognized that their traditional way of life was being rapidly and totally undermined by the introduction of Christianity; it was an important factor in the virtual destruction of the powerful Huron confederacy who, within less than two decades, were forced to abandon their traditional homelands.[57]

Missionaries and the Western Tribes

This was a pattern which was to be replicated as missionaries turned their attention to more western tribes who, seeing much common ground

between their own religion and that of the missionaries who were attempting to convert them, tended to accept various aspects of the Christian teachings. Several western tribes had early on gained some knowledge of Catholicism, long before the missionaries arrived, for as early as 1811, Iroquois fur hunters had migrated from the region of Montreal to the northern Rockies and intermarried with the Salishan and other tribes in the region.[58] These men brought with them an 'Indianized Catholicism, woven from the recollections of their own experience under the Jesuits who had missionized in eastern Canada'.[59] These experiences would certainly include the memories that the literate missionaries were capable, and often willing, to act as interpreters and mediators in trade and treaty transactions.[60] Thus, there were several practical as well as spiritual advantages of embracing the missionaries who were dedicated, generally well-educated, men who not only knew the white world which was impacting on the lives of the Indians, but could help them in communicating their concerns. In the 1830s, no less than four delegations of Nez Perce, Salish and Indians of Iroquois descent from the Plateau regions of the Rocky Mountains, journeyed across the Plains to St. Louis 'in order

to obtain a new spiritual power, or medicine'.[61] This 'supernatural power' was actively sought, 'even at the risk of the apocalyptic destruction hinted at by their prophets'.[62]

'Shining Shirt was given a vision about the future. He prophesied the coming of fair-skinned men wearing long black robes who would teach the Indians a new way of praying and a new moral law. The Black Robes would bring peace, he predicted, but their arrival would also mean the beginning of the end of all the people who then inhabited the land'.

SHINING SHIRT, SALISH PROPHET.[63]

Foremost among those missionaries who responded to the delegations was the young Jesuit, Pierre De Smet and in 1840 with one of the Iroquois delegates as a guide, he made an exploratory visit to the interior Salish; the following year he brought other Jesuit priests, Nicolas Point and Gregory Mengarini, and three Jesuit lay brothers. Remotely situated and isolated the peaceful Salish were viewed as a chosen people by the Jesuits.

The Jesuits' first years among these Plateau tribes were very successful and De Smet reported enthusiastically on devoted Indians 'who gathered from dawn to dusk to hear the Jesuits recite the Great Prayer, learn their catechism, and sing European hymns . . .' He observed, 'The nation of the Flatheads appear to be a chosen people – "the elect of God" . . . Among them, dissensions, quarrels, injuries, and enmities are unknown'.[64]

There is little doubt that the religious world of the missionary and that of the Indians found much common ground. 'Many aspects of Catholic symbology and liturgy such as chants, devotional prayers. . . sacred objects and colors, the use of water and incense for purification . . . ritual processions, the sacred guardians, and religious specialists had strong parallels in the religion and cosmos of the Plains [and Plateau] tribes' among whom De Smet and his colleagues worked.[65]

More than a century after the activities of the Jesuits amonst the Huron, Franciscan missionaries were very busy among the tribes of California. Conquered natives were converted and taken into missions (left) which were built by the Indians themselves at the direction of the Spanish priests as part of a deliberate colonial policy to deal with native peoples in New Spain. The missions caused grave harm to native culture – not to mention life – but they often compared well with later reservation policy.

This grouping (left) of Catholic priest and Passamaquoddy elders appears benign enough, but perhaps it is significant that the youth stands closest to the priest for it was by capturing the interest – or forcing it – of the young that the bonds with the past and the traditional beliefs were broken, very often never to be reforged.

A traditional tree burial (below) for a deceased Sioux near Fort Laramie in about 1868. It was the traditional pre-missionary Sioux practice to wrap their dead in a buffalo robe. It was then placed high in a tree or upon a burial scaffold erected specifically for that purpose. The reason for this probably stems from a desire to protect the body from coyotes and wolves, given that they had no means to dig a deep grave and sufficient rocks were not always available on the Plains.

De Smet, and others like him, worked ceaselessly among the western tribes and in June 1868, nearly 30 years after his first visit to the Salish, he met up with the Teton Sioux on the Powder River. Here, he advanced Christian religious symbolism several stages beyond preaching and waving banners, for now De Smet blessed many children, baptized a number of warriors and gave a crucifix of brass and wood to Sitting Bull – one of a number that he gave to influential Plains leaders.

Betrayed Trust

Conversion of American Indians to Christianity, however, was no easy matter and generally Christianity simply added to, but did not replace, their ways of thinking about the sacred. Jesus and the Saints tended to be viewed as additional guardian spirits; songs and ritual as evoking the supernatural powers.[66] These attitudes were widespread, and thus those Pueblo people who were under the influence of the Catholic missions, early founded in the Southwest, protected tradi-

tional religious beliefs from extinction. They simply 'allowed the church to persist and they incorporated Indian things into it'.[67]

Great conflict and confusion often occurred as the missionaries extended their activities to other tribes. For example, when the Jesuits attempted to end the relentless battles between the Salish and Blackfeet by establishing a mission among the Blackfeet 'The Salish felt betrayed. Christian medicine power brought them victory in war; now the Black Robes were sharing the power with their enemies . . . hopes that Christian power would bring [the Salish] success in hunting and in war eventually brought conflict with the priests, who wanted them to stay at home and farm'.[68]

Cherokee, Creek, Choctaw and to some extent Seminole, followed the teachings and advice of the missionaries and shortly after 1800 missionary and educational activities were well-established among these people. In 1821 *Sequoya* invented the Cherokee alphabet and on its official approval by the tribal leaders, it was adopted by the Cherokee people. The alphabet was accepted with so much enthusiasm that within a few months, thousands of Cherokee were able both to read and write their own language. By 1828, the 'Cherokee Phoenix', a weekly newspaper, was being published in both Cherokee and English. . . within the space of a few years, the tribe was raised to the rank of a literary people.

The relative prosperity was short-lived, however, with the discovery of gold by white prospectors. Even though the deposits were within the limits of Cherokee territory, there was powerful agitation for their removal and the Cherokee were forced to sell their remaining lands east of the Mississippi and forced to join the other three great southeastern tribes – the Creek, Choctaw and Seminole – in Indian Territory (present-day Oklahoma). The removal – with a military escort – took place in the winter of 1838-39: of the 13,000 Cherokee emigrants, fewer than 10,000 reached their destination having faced 'indescribable hardships'. The ordeal became known as 'The Trail of Tears'.[69]

Last Stands

Rather than accepting the inevitable, many tribes of the Plains and Plateau chose confrontation, hence the great Indian Wars of the 1860s to 1890 when Kiowa, Comanche and Apache of the southern Plains and Southwest, and Sioux, Cheyenne and Arapaho of the central Plains, made an heroic stand to stem the white flood.[70] The Blackfeet attempted negotiation, the great chief, Crowfoot, pleading 'with the commissioners not to deceive him'.[71]

Sitting Bull, however, seeing the hopelessness of the Lakota, retreated to Canada in March 1877, joining some 2,000 American Indians who sought refuge from the destruction in the south.[72]

Likewise, in October and November of 1877, Nez Perce Indians under White Bird, crossed the Canadian border, remnants of heroic Nez Perce who after a 1,600-mile (2,575km) epic retreat, were forced to surrender at the Bear Paw Mountains in October 1877. This peaceable tribe, among the first encountered by explorers and missionaries in the early years of the 19th century, had sought freedom and justice in the Grandmother's land. Their tragic surrender summed up in a speech credited to one of their admirable leaders, Joseph, underlined the great sorrow and loss of all American Indians: 'Hear me, my chiefs; . . . my heart is sick and sad. From where the sun now stands, I will fight no more forever!'[73]

All these were patterns which had been replicated many times in the westward expansion. Individuals, tribes, indeed whole cultural areas, thrown into an anomic state, the economic and spiritual base of their lives being changed forever.

Epilogue

In 1989, acknowledging that the encounter almost 500 years ago between Europeans and the Native Americans formed the foundation both for upheaval and for new definitions of history in the lives and perspectives of both groups, the then President of the United States, George Bush, signed legislation that launched a massive program to inspire 'an exponential increase in Native American studies',[74] so that the nation will go forward with a 'new and richer understanding of the heritage, culture, and values of the peoples of the Americas of Indian ancestry'.[75] The legislation established a National Museum of the American Indian as a living memorial dedicated to the collection, preservation, study and exhibition of American Indian languages, literature, history, art and culture and was to be both national and international in its reach. Its first director, W. Richard West Jr., of Cheyenne and Arapaho descent, accepted the commitment to foster a deeper understanding of the meaning of American Indian life and culture.[76]

A new era has dawned: as Sitting Bull once said

'Come, my brothers, let us see what kind of world we make for our children'.[77]

Kicking Bear brought the Ghost Dance to the encampment of the great Hunkpapa Sioux spiritual leader, Sitting Bull, in August of 1890. This knife (left) is said to have belonged to *Tatan'ka iyo' take*, as Sitting Bull was known in his native tongue.
Kicking Bear had been south to Nevada to find out more about the movement sweeping the tribes; the Ghost Dance shirt (above) belonged to an Arapaho follower in 1889 and displays traditional tribal imagery such as the turtle which symbolizes regenerative powers.

BIBLIOGRAPHY

Agent, D. 'LaFlesche Papers Reveal Osage Intellect and Logic' in *Smithsonian Runner,* No 92-4, Smithsonian Institution, Washington D.C. 1992.

Arima, E and Dewhirst, J. 'Nootkans of Vancouver Island' in Suttles, W. (ed.) *Handbook of North American Indians: Vol. 7*, Washington D.C., 1990.

Bahti, T. *Southwestern Indian Arts and Crafts*, Flagstaff, Arizona, 1964

Bahti, T. *Southwestern Indian Ceremonials*, Las Vegas, Nevada, 1970.

Bailey, G.A. (ed.) 'The Osage and The Invisible World' in *The Civilisation of the American Indian Series: Vol. 217*, Norman, Oklahoma, 1995.

Bates, C.D. 'California' in Taylor, C.F. (ed.) *Native American Myths and Legends*, London, 1994.

Beals, R.L. 'Ethnology of the Nisenan' in *University of California Publications in American Archaeology and Ethnology,* 31(6), Berkeley, California, 1933.

Bean, L.J. and Theodoratus, D. 'Western Pomo and Northeastern Pomo' in Heizer, R.F. (ed.) *Handbook of North American Indians: Vol. 8*, Washington D.C., 1978.

Benedict, R.F 'Configurations of Culture in North America' in *American Anthropologist*, Vol. XXXIV. 1932.

Berlandier, J.L. in Ewers, J.C. (ed.) *The Indians of Texas in 1830*, Washington D.C.,1969.

Bishop, M. *Champlain: The Life of Fortitude*, London, 1949.

Blackman, M.B. 'Haida: Traditional Culture' in Suttles, W. (ed.) *Handbook of North American Indians: Vol. 7*, Washington D.C., 1990.

Boas, F. 'Eskimo of Baffin Land and Hudson Bay' in *Bulletin of the American Museum of Natural History*, Vol 15, New York, 1901.

Boas, F. (ed.) *45th Annual Report of the Bureau of American Ethnology*, Smithsonian Institution, Washington D.C., 1930.

Boller, H.A. in Quaife, M.M. (ed.) *Among the Indians: Four Years on the Upper Missouri, 1858-1862*, Lincoln, Nebraska, 1972 (reprint).

Bourke, J.G. 'The Medicine-men of the Apache' in *9th Annual Report of the Bureau of American Ethnology 1887-1888*, Smithsonian Insitution, Washington D.C., 1892.

Bowers, A.W. *Mandan Social and Ceremonial Organization*, Chicago, 1950.

Bowers, A.W. *Hidatsa Social and Ceremonial Organization*, Bureau of American Ethnology. Bulletin 194, Smithsonian Institution, Washington D.C., 1965.

Bright, W. 'Karok' in Heizer, R.F. (ed.) *Handbook of North American Indians: Vol.8*, Washington D.C., 1978.

Brotherston, G. *Image of the New World: The American Continent Portrayed in Native Texts*, London, 1979.

Burch, E.S. Jnr 'Kotzebue Sound Eskimo' in Damas, D. (ed.) *Handbook of North American Indians: Vol. 5*, Washington D.C., 1984.

Callender, C. 'Fox' in Trigger, B.G. (ed.) *Handbook of North American Indians: Vol.15*, Washington D.C., 1978.

Catlin, G. *Letters and Notes on the Manners, Customs and Condition of the North American Indians,* (2 Vols), London, 1841.

Catlin, G. *North American Indians,* (2 Vols), Edinburgh, 1926.

Catlin, G. *Indian Art in Pipestone,* (Ewers, J.C. ed.), Washington D.C., 1979.

Cinq-Mars, J. and Martin, C.A. 'History of Archeological Research in the Subarctic Shield and Mackenzie Valley' in Helm, J. (ed.) *Handbook of North American Indians: Vol.6*, Washington D.C., 1981.

Clark, Capt. W.P. *The Indian Sign Language*, Philadelphia, 1885.

Clarke, N.T. 'The Wampum Belt Collection of the New York State Museum' in *24th Report of the Directors, New York State Museum, Bulletin 288*, Albany, 1931.

Conisbee, L.R. (ed.) *Bedfordshire Bibliography*, Bedfordshire Historical Record Society, 1962.

Connell, E.S. *Son of the Morning Star: General Custer and the Battle of Little Bighorn*, London, 1985.

Copway, G. *The Life, Letters & Speeches of Kah-ge-ga-gah-bowh or G. Copway*, New York, 1850.

Corbusier, W.H. 'Dakota Winter-Count' in N.A.A., Ms.2372, Box 12, Washington, c1880.

Cordell, L.S. 'Prehistory: Eastern Anasazi' in Ortiz, A. (ed.) *Handbook of North American Indians: Vol. 9*, Washington D.C., 1979.

Culin, S. *Games of the North American Indians*, 24th Annual Report of the Bureau of American Ethnology, 1902-03, Smithsonian Institution, Washington D.C., 1907. (Reprint New York, 1975.)

Cumming, W.P.(ed) *The Discoveries of John Lederer*, Charlottesville and Winston-Salem, 1958.

Curtis, E.S. *The North American Indian*, (Hodge, F.W. ed.), London, 1909.

Cushing, F.H. *Zuni Fetishes*, 1883. (Reprinted Flagstaff, Arizona, 1970.)

DeMalle, R.J. and Lavenda, R.H. 'Wakan: Plains Siouan Concepts of Power' in Fogelson, R.D. & Adams, R. (eds.) *The Anthroplology of Power,* New York, 1977.

Dempsey, H.A. 'A Blackfoot Winter Count', *Occasional Paper No 1*, Glenbow Foundation, Calgary, Alberta, 1965.

Dempsey, H.A. *Crowfoot Chief of the Blackfeet*, Norman, Oklahoma, 1972.

Denig, E.T. 'Of The Crow Nation' in Ewers, J.C. (ed.) *Anthropological Papers No 33*, Bureau of American Ethnology, Smithsonian Institution, Washington D.C., 1953.

Densmore, F. *Teton Sioux Music*, Bureau of American Ethnology, Bulletin 61, Smithsonian Institution, Washington D.C., 1918.

Densmore, F. *Mandan and Hidatsa Music,* Bureau of American Ethnology, Bulletin 80, Smithsonian Institution, Washington D.C., 1923.

Densmore, F. *Yuman and Yaqui Music*, Bureau of American Ethnology, Bulletin 110, Smithsonian Institution, Washington D.C., 1932.

Densmore, F. *Nootka and Quileute Music*, Bureau of American Ethnology, Bulletin 124, Smithsonian Institution, Washington D.C., 1939.

Densmore, F. *Technique in the Music of the American Indian*, Anthropology Papers No. 36, Bureau of American Ethnology, Bulletin 151, Smithsonian Institution, Washington D.C., 1953 (a).

Densmore, F. *The Belief of the Indian in a Connection between Song and the Supernatural*, Anthropology Papers No. 37, Bureau of American Ethnology, Bulletin 151, Smithsonian Institution, Washington D.C., 1953 (b).

Densmore, F. *Chippewa Customs*, Bureau of American Ethnology, Bulletin 86, Smithsonian Institution, Washington D.C., 1929. (Reprinted St. Paul, Minnesota, 1979.)

Dodge, Col. R.I. *33 Years Among our Wild Indians*, New York, 1882.

Donaldson, T. Appendix (Part V) in *Annual Report of the Smithsonian Institution to July 1885*, Washington D.C., 1886.

Dorsey, G.A. *The Arapaho Sun Dance; The Ceremony of the Offerings Lodge*, Field Columbian Museum, Publication 75, Anthropology Series, Vol. IV, Chicago, 1903.

Dorsey, G.A. *Traditions of the Skidi Pawnee*, Memoirs of the American Folk-Lore Society 8, Boston and New York, 1904.

Downing, G.R. and Furniss, L.S. 'Some Observations on Camas Digging and Baking among Present-Day Nez Perce' in *Tebiwa: The Journal of the Idaho State University Museum*, Vol. 11, No 1, Pocatello, Idaho, 1968.

Driscoll, B. 'Pretending to be Caribou' in McClelland and Stewart (eds.) *The Spirit Sings*, Toronto, 1987.

Dubois, D. and Berger, Y. *Les Indiens des Plaines*, Neuilly-sur-Seine, 1978.

Eastman, C.A. *Indian Boyhood*, New York, 1902.

Eccles, W.J. 'The Fur Trade in the Colonial Northeast' in Washburn, W.E. (ed.) *Handbook of North American Indians: Vol.4*, Washington D.C., 1988.

Elsasser, A.B. 'Mattole, Nongate, Sinkyone, Lassik, and Wailaki' in Heizer, R.F. (ed.) *Handbook of North American Indians: Vol.8*, Washington D.C., 1978.

Evans, M.A. *Indian Loving Catlin*, 1930.

Ewers, J.C. *Plains Indian Painting*, Stanford University, California, 1939.

Ewers, J.C. *Blackfeet Crafts*, Haskell Institute, Lawrence, 1945.

Ewers, J.C. *The Horse in Blackfoot Indian Culture*, Bureau of American Ethnology, Bulletin 159. Smithsonian Institution, Washington D.C., 1955.

Ewers, J.C. *Early White Influence Upon Plains Indian Painting*, Smithsonian Miscellaneous Collections, Vol. 134, No. 7, Washington D.C., 1957.

Ewers, J.C. *The Blackfeet: Raiders on the Northwestern Plains*, Norman, Oklahoma, 1958.

Ewers, J.C. *When Red and White Men Met*, reprinted from *The Western Historical Quarterly*, Vol. II, No. 2, 1971.

Ewers, J.C. *The Use of Artifacts and Pictures in the Study of Plains Indian History, Art, and Religion*, reprinted from the *Annals of the New York Academy of Sciences*, Vol. 376, New York, 1981.

Ewers, J.C. *Plains Indian Sculpture: Traditional Art from America's Heartland*, Washington D.C., 1986.

Farabee, W.C. 'Indian Cradles' in *The Museum Journal,* No.11:4, University of Pennsylvania, Philadephia, 1920.

Feest, C.F. *Indianer Nordamerikas*, Museum für Volkerkunde, Wien, 1968.

Feest, C.F. 'Another French Account of Virginia Indians by John Lederer' in *The Virginia Magazine of History and Biography*, Vol. 83, No. 2, 1975.

Feest, C.F. Essay in Macgregor, A. (ed.) *Tradescant Rarities*, Oxford, 1983.

Fenton, W.N. 'Northern Iroquoian Culture Patterns' in Trigger, B.G. (ed.) *Handbook of North American Indians: Vol. 15*, Washington D.C., 1978.

Flannery, R. *The Gros Ventres of Montana: Part I: Social Life*, Anthropological Series No. 15, The Catholic University of America Press, Washington D.C., 1953.

Fletcher, A.C. and La Flesche, F. 'The Omaha Tribe' in *27th Annual Report of the Bureau of American Ethnology*, Smithsonian Institution, Washington D.C., 1911.

Fowler, C.S. 'Subsistence' in D'Azevedo, W.L. (ed.) *Handbook of North American Indians: Vol. 11*, Washington D.C., 1986.

Freuchen, P. *Book of the Eskimos*, Greenwich, Connecticut, 1961.

Frigout, A. 'Hopi Ceremonial Organization' in Ortiz, A. (ed.) *Handbook of North American Indians: Vol .9*, Washington D.C., 1979.

Garbarino, M.S. in Porter III, F.W. (ed.) *The Seminole*, New York and Philadelphia, 1989.

Gibson, J.R. 'The Maritime Trade of the North Pacific Coast' in Washburn, W. (ed.) *Handbook of North American Indians: Vol.4*, Washington D.C., 1988.

Gilman, C. and Schneider, M.J. *The Way to Independence*, St.Paul, Minnesota, 1987.

Gilmore, R. 'The Northern Arapaho Cradle' in *American Indian Art Magazine*, Vol.16, No.1, Scottsdale, Arizona, 1990.

Goldfrank, E.S (ed.) *Isleta Paintings*, Washington D.C., 1970.

Green, R. in Porter III, F.W. (ed.) *Women in American Indian Society*, New York and Philadelphia, 1992.

Grinnell, G.B. *Blackfoot Lodge Tales*, London, 1893.

Grinnell, G.B. *The Story of the Indian*, London, 1896.

Grinnell, G.B. *The Cheyenne Indians: Their History and Ways of Life*, (2 Vols.), New Haven, Connecticut, 1923.

Grinnell, G.B. *By Cheyenne Campfires*, New Haven, Connecticut, 1926.

Hamilton, T.M. *Native American Bows*, Missouri Archaeological Society Special Publications, No. 5, Columbia, Missouri, 1982.

Hardesty, Wm. *The Loucheux Indians*, Smithsonian Institution Report 1866, Washington D.C., 1867.

Hariot, T. *Narrative of the first English Plantation of Virginia*, London, 1893.

Harrington, M.R. *The Indians of New Jersey: Dickon Among the Lenapes*, New Brunswick, New Jersey, 1938. (Reprinted 1963.)

Hartmann, H. *Kachina-Figuren der Hopi-Indianer*, Museum für Volkerkunde, Berlin, 1978.

Heidenreich, C.E. 'Huron' in Trigger, B.G. (ed.) *Handbook of North American Indians: Vol.15*, Washington D.C., 1978.

Hickerson, H. *The Chippewa and their Neighbors: A Study in Ethnohistory*, New York, 1970.

Higbee, R. 'Encounters in New Mexico' in *Smithsonian Runner*, No 92-4, July-August, Smithsonian Institution, Washington D.C., 1992.

Hilger, Sister M. Inez *Chippewa Child Life and its Cultural Background*, Bureau of American Ethnology, Bulletin 146, Smithsonian Institution, Washington D.C., 1951.

Hilger, Sister M. Inez *Arapaho Child Life and its Background*, Bureau of American Ethnology, Bulletin 148, Smithsonian Institution, Washington D.C., 1952.

Hodge, F.W. (ed.) *Handbook of American Indians North of Mexico*, (2 Vols.), Washington D.C., 1907 - 1910.

Hoffman, W.J. *The Midewiwin or Grand Medicine Socity of the Ojibwa,* Bureau of American Ethnology, 7th Annual Report 1885-86, Smithsonian Institution, Washington D.C., 1891.

Hoffman, W.J. *The Menomini Indians*, Bureau of American Ethnology, 14th Annual Report, Smithsonian Institution, Washington D.C., 1896.

Holm, B. 'Art' in Suttles, W. (ed.) *Handbook of North American Indians: Vol.7*, Washington D.C., 1990.

Howard, J.H. *Dakota Winter Counts as a Source of Plains History*, Anthropological Papers, No. 61, Bureau of American Ethnology, Bulletin 173, Smithsonian Institution, Washington D.C., 1960.

Howard, J.H. *The British Museum Winter Count*, British Museum Occasional Paper No. 4, Department of Ethnography, London, 1979.

Hultkrantz, A.'Mythology and Religious Concepts' in D'Azevedo, W.L. (ed.) *Handbook of North American Indians: Vol.11*, Washington D.C., 1986.

Hulton, P. *America 1585. The Complete Drawings of John White*, London, 1984.

Hume, I.N. 'No Fayre Lady: The Several Faces of Pocahontas' in *Colonial Williamsburg,* Autumn 1994.

Indiana Historical Society (Black, G.A. et al) *Walam Olum*, Indianapolis, 1954.

Jablow, J. *The Cheyenne in Plains Indian Trade Relations 1795-1840*, Seattle and London, 1950.

Jenness, D. 'Indians of Canada' in *Bulletin 65, Anthropological Series No.15*, National Museum of Canada, Ottawa, 1932. (Reprinted 1980.)

Jonaitis, A. *From the Land of the Totem Poles*, London, 1988.

Kennedy, D.I.D. & Bouchard R.T. 'Bella Coola'in Suttles, W. (ed.) *Handbook of North American Indians: Vol. 7*, Washington D.C., 1990.

Kenton, E. (ed.) *Black Gown and Redskins*, London, 1956.

Klaus, F.W. *A Survey of American Indian Rock Art*, Graz, Austria. 1979.

Kroeber, A.L. *The Arapaho*, Bulletin of the American Museum of Natural History 1902 and 1907. Reprinted Lincoln, Nebraska, and London 1983.

Lafitau, J.F. in Fenton, W.N. and Moore, E.M. (eds.) *Customs of the American Indians*, Toronto, 1977.

Laguna, F. de 'Tlingit' in Suttles, W. (ed.) *Handbook of North American Indians: Vol.7*, Washington D.C., 1990.

Landy, D. 'Tuscarora Among the Iroquois' in Trigger, B.G. (ed.) *Handbook of North American Indians: Vol.15*, Washington D.C., 1978.

La Vonne Brown Ruoff, A. *American Indian Literatures*, The Modern Language Association of America, New York, 1990.

Lewis, M and Clark W. in Thwaites, R.G. (ed.) *The Original Journals of Lewis and Clark, 1804-1806*, (8 Vols.), New York, 1904-1905 (Reprinted 1959.)

Lewis, M.G. 'Indian Maps: Their Place in the History of Plains Cartography' in *Great Plains Quarterly*, Spring, Norman, Oklahoma, 1984.

Lewis, M.G. 'Indicators of Unacknowledged Assimilations from Amerindian Maps' in *Imago Mundi*, Kings College, London, 1986.

Lewis, M.G. Personal correspondence to the author, University of Sheffield, 1988 & 1989.

Lowie, R.H. *Myths and Traditions of the Crow Indians*, Anthropology Papers of the American Museum of Natural History, New York, Vol. XXV Part 1, 1918.

Lowie, R.H. The Crow Indians, New York, 1935.

Lyford, C.A. *Iroquois Crafts*, Lawrence, Kansas, 1945.

Macfarlan, A & P. *Handbook of American Indian Games*, New York, 1958.

Mallery, G *Pictographs of the North American Indians*, 4th Annual Report of the Bureau of American Ethnology, Washington D.C., 1886.

Mallery, G *Picture Writing of the American Indians*, 10th Annual Report of the Bureau of American Ethnology, Washington D.C., 1893.

Mark, J. *Four Anthropologists: An American Science in its Early Years*, New York, 1980.

Marquis, T.H. *Memoirs of a White Crow Indian*, New York, 1928.

Mary-Rousselière, G. 'Iglulik' in Damas, D. (ed.) *Handbook of North American Indians: Vol. 5*, Washington D.C., 1984.

Mason, O.T. 'Cradles of the American Aborigines' in *Annual Report of the United States National Museum for 1887*, Washington D.C., 1889.

Maximilian, Prince of Wied. 'Early Western Travels 1748-1846, Vols. XXII and XXIII.' in Thwaites, R.G. (ed.), Cleveland, Ohio, 1906.

McCary, B.C. *Indians in Seventeenth-Century Virginia*, Charlottesville, 1957.

McCartney A.P. 'Prehistory of the Aleutian Region' in Damas, D. (ed.) *Handbook of North American Indians: Vol. 5*, Washington D.C., 1984.

McKee J.O. *The Choctaw*, New York & Philadelphia, 1989.

Mooney, J. 'The Sacred Formulas of the Cherokees' in

Annual Report of the Bureau of American Ethnology (1885-86), Washington D.C., 1891.
Mooney, J. 'The Ghost Dance Religion and the Sioux Outbreak of 1890' in *14th Annual Report of The Bureau of American Ethnology*, (2 Vols.), Washington D.C., 1896.
Mooney, J. 'Calendar History of the Kiowa Indians' in 17th Annual Report of The Bureau of American Ethnology, 1898, Reprinted 1979 with Introduction by John C. Ewers, Washington D.C.
Moore, J.H. *A Study of Religious Symbolism among the Cheyenne Indians*. Ph.D Thesis, New York University, 1974.
Morgan, L.H. in Lloyd, H.M. (ed.) *League of the Ho-dé-no-sau-nee or Iroquois* (1851), (2 Vols.), New York, 1901.
Morgan, L.H. *Houses and House Life of the American Aborigines*, Chicago, 1965. (Originally published in 1881 as Vol. IV of *Contributions to North American Ethnology*, Washington D.C.)
Nabokov, P. and Easton, R. 'Heye Foundation Returns Iroquois Wampum Belts' in *Northeast Indian Quarterly,* Vol. V, No. 2, Summer., Ithaca, New York, 1988.
Nabokov, P and Easton, R. *Native American Architecture*, New York and Oxford, 1989.
Petersen, R. 'East Greenland Before 1950' in Damas, D. (ed.) *Handbook of North American Indians: Vol. 5*, Washington D.C., 1984.
Peterson, H.L. *American Indian Tomahawks*, Museum of The American Indian, Heye Foundation, New York, 1971.
Peterson, J. *Sacred Encounters*, (The De Smet Project, Washington State University), Norman, Oklahoma, 1993.
Porter, J.C. *Paper Medicine Man: John Gregory Bourke and his American West*, Norman, Oklahoma, 1986.
Powell, J.V 'Quileute' in Suttles, W. (ed.) *Handbook of North American Indians: Vol.7*, Washington D.C., 1990.
Powers, S. 'Tribes of California' in *Contributions to North American Ethnology 3*, U.S. Geographical and Geological Survey of the Rocky Mountain Region, Washington D.C., 1877.
Powers, W.K. *Sacred Language*, Norman, Oklahoma, 1986.
Rasmussen, W.M.S. and Tilton, R.S. *Pocahontas: Her Life & Legend*, Richmond, Virginia, 1994.
Ray, D.J. 'Bering Strait Eskimo' in Damas, D. (ed.) *Handbook of North American Indians: Vol.5*, Washington D.C., 1984.
Reichard, G.A. *Navajo Medicine Man Sandpaintings*, New York, 1977.
Riggs, T.L. 'Sunset to Sunset' in *Report and Historical Collections of the South Dakota State Historical Society XXIX*, 1958.
Ritzenthaler, R.E. 'The Potawatomi Indians of Wisconsin' in Milwaukee Public Museum Bulletin, Vol. 19, No.3, Milwaukee, 1953.
Ritzenthaler, R.E. and Ritzenthaler, P. *The Woodland Indians of the Western Great Lakes*, New York, 1970.
Robinson, E. 'Evidence Suggests Cancer Cure in Essiac' in *Planetary Connections*, Autumn, Evesham, Worcestershire, 1993.
Scudiere, P.J. 'The Iroquois Collection of the New York State Museum' in *American Indian Art Magazine*, Scottsdale, Arizona, 1981.
Seaver, J.E. *The Life of Mary Jemison*, New York, 1982.
Secoy, F.R. *Changing Military Patterns on the Great Plains*, Seattle, 1953.
Seger, J.H. in Vestal, S. (ed.) *Early Days Among the Cheyenne and Arapahoe Indians*, Norman, Oklahoma, 1956.
Sheehan, C. 'Moment of Death: Gift of Life. A Reinterpretation of the Northwest Coast Image "Hawk" ' in *Anthropologica. N.S.*, Vol XX, Nos. 1-2, 1978.
Sheehan, C. 'The Northwest Coast' in Taylor, C.F. (ed.) *Native American Myths and Legends*, London, 1994.
Silver, S. 'Shastan Peoples' in Heizer, R.F. (ed.) *Handbook of North American Indians: Vol. 8*, Washington D.C., 1978.
Skinner, A. 'Notes on the Eastern Cree and Northern Saulteaux' in *Anthropology Papers of the American Museum of Natural History*, Vol. IX, Part 1, New York, 1911.
Smith, D. *Indian Experiences*, Caldwell, Idaho, 1943.
Smith, D.B. *Sacred Feathers: The Reverend Peter Jones (Kahkewaquonaby) and the Mississauga Indians*, Toronto and London, 1987.
Smith, J.G.E. 'Economic Uncertainty in an "Original Affluent Society:" Caribou and Caribou Eater Chipewyan Adaptive Strategies' in *Arctic Anthropology* 15(1), 1978.
Smith, J.G.E. 'Chipewyan' in Helm, J. (ed.) *Handbook of North American Indians: Vol. 6*, Washington D.C., 1981.
Smith, M.W. 'Mandan History as reflected in Butterfly's Winter Count' in *Ethnohistory*, Vol. 7, No. 3, Summer, Buffalo, New York, 1960.
Space, R.S. *The Lolo Trail*, Lewiston, Idaho. 1970.
Speck, F.G. *Naskapi: The Savage Hunters of the Labrador Peninsular*, Norman, Oklahoma, 1935. (Reprinted 1977.)
Speck, F.G. *The Iroquois*, Cranbrook Institute of Science Bulletin 23, Bloomfield Hills, Michigan. 1945.
Spencer, R.F. *The North Alaskan Eskimo*, Bureau of American Ethnology Bulletin 171, Smithsonian Institution, Washington D.C., 1959.
Spinden, H.J. *The Nez Perce Indians*, Memoirs of the American Anthropological Association, Vol. II: Part 3, 1908. (Reprinted New York 1974.)
Stewart, F.H. 'Mandan and Hidatsa Villages in the Eighteenth and Nineteenth Centuries' in *Plains Anthropologist*, 19-66, Pt. 1, 1974.
Stewart, T.D. *The People of America*, London, 1973.
Sturtevant, W.C. 'Iroquois Hieroglyphics', Paper - 10th American Indian Workshop, Vienna, Austria, 1989.
Sturtevant, W.C. and Taylor, C.F (eds.) *The Native Americans*, London. 1991.
Suttles, W. 'Central Coast Salish' in Suttles, W. (ed.) *Handbook of North American Indians: Vol.7*, Washington D.C., 1990.
Suttles, W. and Lane, B. 'Southern Coast Salish' in Suttles, W. (ed.) *Handbook of North American Indians: Vol.7*, Washington D.C., 1990.
Swagerty, W.R. 'Indian Trade in the Trans-Mississippi West to 1870' in Washburn, W. (ed.) *Handbook of North American Indians: Vol.4*, Washington D.C., 1988.
Swanton, J.R. 'Contributions to the ethnology of the Haida (of Queen Charlotte Islands)', *Jessup North Pacific Expedition, Vol. 5, Pt. I, American Museum of Natural History, Bulletin 29*, New York, 1905.
Swanton, J.R. *Source Material for the Social and Ceremonial Life of the Choctaw Indians*, Bureau of American Ethnology, Bulletin 103, Smithsonian Institution, Washington D.C., 1931.
Taylor, C.F. *The* O-kee-pa *and Four Bears: An Insight into Mandan Ethnology*, The English Westerners Society, Vol. 15, No. 3, London, 1973.
Taylor C.F. *The Warriors of the Plains*, London, 1975.
Taylor C.F. Title essay in Johnson, B.C. (ed.) *Ho For The Great West! The Silver Jubilee Publication of the English Westerners' Society*, London, 1980.
Taylor C.F. 'Wakanyan: Symbols of Power and Ritual of the Teton Sioux' in McCaskill, D. (ed.) *Amerindian Cosmology, Cosmos 4, Yearbook of the Traditional Cosmology Society, The Canadian Journal of Native Studies*, Brandon, Manitoba, 1989.
Taylor C.F. *Saam: The Symbolic Content of Early Northern Plains Ceremonial Regalia*, Wyk auf Foehr, Germany. 1993.
Taylor C.F. 'Taku Skanskan. Power symbols of the Universe: parallels in the Cosmos of Plains Indians and White Missionaries' in *The Artist & The Missionary. The Proceedings of the 1992 Plains Indian Seminar*, Buffalo Bill Historical Center, Cody, Wyoming, 1994(a).
Taylor C.F. (ed.) *Native American Myths and Legends*, London. 1994(b).
Taylor C.F. *The Plains Indians*, London. 1994(c).
Taylor C.F. *Wapa'ha: The Plains Feathered Headdress (Die Plains Federhaube*, Wyk auf Foehr, Germany, 1994(d).
Taylor C.F. (ed.) *Native American Arts and Crafts*, London, 1995.
Taylor C.F. *Sunka Wakan: Sacred Horses of the Plains Indians. Ethos and Regalia*, Wyk auf Foehr, Germany, 1995(b).
Tedlock, D. 'Zuni Religion and World View' in Ortiz, A. (ed.) *Handbook of North American Indians: Vol. 9*, Washington D.C., 1979.
Teit, J.A. 'The Salishan Tribes of the Western Plateaus' in Boas, F. (ed.) *45th Annual Report of the Bureau of American Ethnology*, Smithsonian Institution, Washington D.C., 1930.
Thompson, D. in Tyrell, J.B. (ed.) *David Thompson's Narrative of his Explorations in Western America, 1784-1812,* Toronto, 1916.
Titiev, M. *Old Oraibi: A Study of the Hopi Indians of Third Mesa*, Albuquerque, New Mexico, 1992.
Tobert, N and Pitt, F. 'The Southwest' in Taylor, C.F. (ed.) *Native American Myths and Legends*, London, 1994.
Tomkins, W. *Universal Indian Sign Language*, San Diego, California, 1926. (Reprinted 1954.)
Tooker, E. 'Iroquois Since 1820' in Trigger, B.G. (ed) *Handbook of North American Indians: Vol. 15*, Washington D.C., 1978.
Tooker, E. 'The League of the Iroquois: Its History, Politics, and Ritual' in Trigger, B.G. (ed) *Handbook of North American Indians: Vol. 15*, Washington D.C., 1978.
Trigger, B.G. 'Early Iroquoian Contacts with Europeans'. in Trigger, B.G. (ed) *Handbook of North American Indians: Vol. 15*, Washington D.C., 1978.
Underhill, R. *Indians of the Pacific Northwest*, Washington D.C., 1945.
Utley, R.M. *Bluecoats and Redskins: The United States Army and the Indian 1866-1891*, London, 1973.
Watson, M.J. 'Deupree Cradle Collection', State Arts Council of Oklahoma, (no date).
Wedel, M.M. and DeMallie, R.J. 'The Ethnohistorical Approach in Plains Area Studies' in Wood, W.R. and Liberty, M. (eds.) *Anthropology on the Great Plains*, Lincoln, Nebraska, 1980.
Wedel, W.R. 'Notes on the Prairie Turnip Among the Plains Indians' in *Nebraska History* (Reprint).Vol. 59, No.2, Nebraska State Historical Society, Lincoln, Nebraska, 1978.
Weist, K.M. 'Plains Indian Women: An Assessment' in Wood, W.R. and Liberty, M. (eds.) *Anthropology on the Great Plains*, Lincoln, Nebraska, 1980.
Wildschut, W. 'Blackfoot Pipe Bundles' in *Indian Notes*, Museum of the American Indian, Vol.5. No.4, Heye Foundation, New York, 1928.
Will, G.F. and Hyde, G.E. *Corn Among the Indians of the Upper Missouri*, Lincoln, Nebraska, 1917. (Reprinted 1964.)
Wilson, G.L. 'Field Report', Vol. 8, Wilson Papers, Minnesota Historical Society, St. Paul, Minnesota, 1909.
Wilson, G.L. 'Field Report', Vol. 10, Wilson Papers, Minnesota Historical Society, St. Paul, 1911.
Wilson, G.L. 'Field Report', Vol. 13, Wilson Papers, Minnesota Historical Society, St. Paul, 1913.
Wilson, G.L. 'Field Report', Vol. 18, Wilson Papers, Minnesota Historical Society, St. Paul, 1915.
Wilson, G.L. 'Agriculture of the Hidatsa Indians: An Indian Interpretation' in *Studies in the Social Sciences*, No. 9. University of Minnesota, Minneapolis. 1917.
Wilson, G.L. 'Field Report', Vol. 22, Wilson Papers, Minnesota Historical Society, St. Paul, 1918.
Wissler, C. *Social Organization and Ritualistic Ceremonies of the Blackfoot Indians. Part II: Ceremonial Bundles of the Blackfoot Indians*, American Museum of Natural History, Vol. VII. New York, 1912.
Wissler, C. 'The Sun Dance of the Blackfoot Indians' in *Anthropology Papers of the American Museum of Natural History*, Vol. XVI, New York, 1918.
Wissler, C. *Indians of the Plains*, New York, 1920.
Wissler, C. *The Relation of Nature to Man in Aboriginal North America*, New York, 1937.
Wissler, C. *Indians of the United States*, New York, 1940.
Wood, W.R. 'Plains Trade in Prehistoric and Protohistoric Intertribal Relations' in Wood, W.R. and Liberty, M. (eds.), *Anthropology on the Great Plains,* Lincoln, Nebraska, 1980.
Wood, W.R. and Liberty, M. (eds.) *Anthropology on the Great Plains*, Lincoln, Nebraska, 1980.
Wood, W.R. and Thiessen, T.D. *Early Fur Trade on the Northern Plains*, Norman, Oklahoma, 1985.
Zolla, E. *The Writer and the Shaman: A Morphology of the American Indian*, New York, 1969. Translated by Rosenthal, R. and Wolff, A.H and K.

REFERENCES

INTRODUCTION

1 See Taylor (ed.),1994 (b) and 1995.
2 See Sturtevant and Taylor,1991.
3 Raleigh called the area Virginia to honor the virgin Queen, Elizabeth I.
4 For a more detailed description of these villages see Hulton, 1984.
5 Pocahontas married John Rolfe; she died in 1618 and is buried at Gravesend, Kent. The so-called Powhatan's Mantle, now at the Asmolean Museum, Oxford, is shown on page 28.
6 Rasmussen and Tilton,1994:30
7 Contacts were also made with the indigenous peoples of the Northwest Coast, Aleutian Islands and Alaska, by Russian fur traders in the mid-18th century. While their prime aim was to barter for sea-otter pelts, the artists who traveled with them documented much of the daily life of the people they encountered. So too in the Southwest when the Spanish arived in the mid-16th century (see Sturtevant and Taylor, 1991).
8 Catlin,1841:Vol.I:4
9 Antonio de Ulloa (1772) in Stewart,1973:55
10 In the 19th century stature varied considerably among the tribes. Thus in parts of California, the Southwest and on the Northwest Coast, the range for males was 5ft 3in-5ft 6in (1.6m-1.65m). However, in the Woodlands and the Plains and Plateau for tribes such as the Iroquois, Chippewa, Winnebago, Osage, Sioux, Crow, Cheyenne, Arapaho and Nez Perce, the height of the adult male ranged between about 5ft 7in to 5ft 9in (1.7m to 1.75m). Among the Cheyenne there were some particularly tall individuals – 20 per cent of those measured in the early 20th century were almost 6ft (1.82m), On average, women were some 5in shorter than men (12.5cm). Wissler,1920:144
11 The Footnotes and Bibliography considerably extend this list.
12 With acknowledgement to L.P. Hartley.

TRIBAL AND SOCIAL ORGANIZATION

1 Copway,1850:24
2 Bright, Heizer (ed.),1978:184-185
3 Powers,1877:21
4 Beals,1933:359-360.
5 Bates, Taylor (ed.),1994:78-81
6 Ray, Damas (ed.),1984:286
7 Powhatan's favorite daughter was the famed *Pocahontas* who was captured by the English and who married John Rolfe in April 1613.
8 McCary,1957:12
9 ibid:11
10 Referring to themselves as *Hasinai*, 'our own folk', evidence suggests that this confederacy was based on much more ancient traditions of alliances between tribes but little is known of the political laws which governed them.
11 Tooker, Trigger (ed.),1978:418
12 The Tuscaroras joined the Iroquois League sometime between September 1722 and May 1723 (Landy, Trigger (ed.),1978:519). The confederacy was then referred to as the 'Six Nations'.
13 Tooker, Trigger (ed.),1978:425
14 Jenness,1932:135-137
15 Tooker, Trigger (ed.),1978:422
16 As Clark Wissler observed, there is some historical evidence that knowledge of the League influenced the colonies in their first efforts to form a confederacy and later to write a constitution (Wissler,1940:112).
17 This was the general name Blackfoot or Blackfeet, the former being the more literal translation of the native name *Siksikauwa* or 'black-footed people' (Ewers,1958:5).
18 Ewers,1958:5
19 Jablow,1950:72-77
20 Wissler,1912
21 Densmore,1918:113
22 Swanton,1905:296
23 Hardesty,1867:312
24 Hearne (1958) in Sturtevant and Taylor,1991:
25 Green, Porter (ed.),1992:89
26 ibid:93
27 ibid:100
28 Married life began in the wife's parents' home. Here, the wife was definite mistress of the household; she could order the husband from the home should the occasion arise and the children were considered hers.

29 Densmore,1918:70
30 Bean and Theodoratus, Heizer (ed.),1978:196
31 Flannery,1953:127-129
32 Hilger,1951:13
33 Hilger,1952:47
34 Hilger,1951:30
35 Arima and Dewhirst, Suttles (ed.),1990:405; Powell, Suttles (ed.),1990:433; Suttles, Suttles (ed.),1990:465
36 Catlin,1926.Vol.II:152
37 Titiev,1992:7
38 (a) There were definite exceptions to this general rule, however. Thus, in the Pueblos, while an individual might bear several names, one name was generally retained throughout life; the Chippewa had a similar custom (Hilger,1951:35). (b) As Ritzenthaler has observed, the acquisition of surnames by the Potawatomi (of the Wisconsin region) was a recent development - within the last 60 years. Many of these were acquired as a result of a need to put Potawatomi Indians on white registers (Ritzenthaler,1953:142).
39 Swanton in Hodge,1910.Part II:17
40 Wrong translations of Indian names were common on the Great Plains during the 19th century and interpreters, even when they had the opportunity to make sharp distinctions, seldom took the trouble to make them. A good example is Old Man or Young Man Afraid of His Horses which is rendered in Lakota as *Ta-Cun-ka Ko-ki-pa-pi*, 'They Fear His Horses' - nothing whatever about 'man', young or old! (See Smith,1943:125)
41 There is an interesting contrast here in lightning symbolism of the Athapascan Navajo who migrated from the far north in about the 15th century, and that of the Pueblo people - ancient inhabitants of the region.
42 Watson,no date:2-3
43 Gilmore,1990:71
44 Hilger,1952:33
45 Kroeber,1902:144 and Hilger,1952:33
46 See Mason,1889:161-212
47 Ritzenthaler,1953:139
48 Tobert and Pitt in Taylor (ed.),1994:39
49 Bahti,1964:20
50 Grinnell,1923,Vol.I:129
51 ibid:130
52 It was believed that if married men lay beside their wives during the menstrual period, 'they were likely to be wounded in their next battle' (ibid).
53 Laguna, Suttles (ed.),1990:210
54 Spencer,1959:244
55 ibid:243
56 ibid:242
57 Beverley, circa 1700 in McCary,1957:64
58 McCary,1957:63
59 See Taylor, Taylor (ed.),1994:53
60 Suttles and Lane, Suttles (ed.),1990:497
61 Hultkrantz, D'Azevedo (ed.),1986:635 The contact with supernatural powers was not limited to teenagers. Both older men and women sought power by visions or dreams (those obtained in a vision were generally considered the more potent). See Suttles and Lane, Suttles (ed.),1990:497 and Callender, Trigger (ed.),1978:643.

KNOWLEDGE

1 Eastman, 1902:42
2 In Feest,1975:156-157
3 Seger, Vestal (ed.),1956:131-132
4 For a discussion of the extensive use of such signs and symbols in the Americas, see Brotherston,1979:particularly pp.13-19.
5 Bourke,1892:550
6 Jesuit Relations,1858:19 Mallery,1893:791 Bourke also reports on the use of medicine cords among the Apache, Navajo and Zuni which were reserved for the most sacred and important occasions. (Bourke,1993 reprint: 102-105)
7 Mallery,1893:227 and Bourke, 1993 (reprint) : 112 (a) The ethnologist, John C. Ewers, recently drew the author's attention to the fact that *Tomocomo*, brother-in-law of *Pocahontas*, was instructed by *Powhatan* to keep a record of the number of people he saw when they docked in Plymouth in June 1616. This he did by cutting notches in a stick; however, it was reported that 'he was quickly wearie of that taske' (Hume,1994:58). (JCE to CFT, Arlington, November 1994)
(b) In 1670, the Oenock of present-day North Carolina were using reeds and straws to record ceremonials and colored knotted strings as well as small wheels which were employed for keeping time. See Cumming (ed.),1958:12-13.
8 Seaver,1982:176-177
9 Sturtevant,1989:12-13
10 This practice was widespread in North America. See, for example, Feest,1968:67.
11 See particularly Ewers,(1939).
12 McCary,1957:58
13 Feest,1983:135
14 One early observer recorded of *Atone*: '(He) makes the sun to shine, creating the moone and starrs his companyons, great powers, and which dwell with him, and by whose virtues and influences the under earth is tempered, and brings forth her fruicts according to her seasons'. (Strachey,c.1613 in McCary,1957:58)
15 As McCary has observed, the structure of the Siouan and Algonquian religions at this date was very similar. (McCary,1957:62)
16 See Feest,1975:157-159
17 Harrington,1938:203-210. The *Walam Olum* proper is divided into five books or songs, each made up of a varying number of verses which total to 183. One major theme was the migration from Asia to Alaska and south and east across North America.
18 See Zolla.1969:233 and Taylor,1994(a):58-59.
19 The word 'east' in Lenape, interestingly, means 'white' (See Brotherston,1979:51).
20 Starting in 1933, a some 20 year study of the *Walam Olum* was initiated by the Indiana Historical Society who established a fellowship at Yale. The conclusion was (in 1954) that the several scholars who cooperated in the study 'have all the confidence in the historical value of the *Walam Olum* that Schliemann had in the accuracy of the Homeric epics'. (Indiana Historical Society, Black et al,1954:xiv)
21 Hickerson,1970:52
22 Hoffman,1891:165
23 An essential feature in the public initiation was the magical 'shooting' of shells into the bodies of the candidates. Referred to as *migis*, the shells – often cowrie – were said to be 'full of a mystic vital force, (which) would drive out the sickness and "renew life"'. (Ritzenthaler,1970:90)
24 Hickerson,1970:52
25 Cass in Mallery,1893:360 The universal aspect of the recording of messages to other parties together with the associated symbolic representation, seems to have been widespread, seemingly well-understood, and crossed several linguistic barriers. In the Plains region, for example, an encounter between the Cheyenne (Algonquian) and Pawnee (Caddoan) was recorded by the Pawnee in charcoal on a stripped log. The Pawnee had completely annihilated the opposition. Later, a party of Sioux (Siouan) found the log; both Sioux and friends of the dead Cheyenne, had no difficulty in understanding the message. (Grinnell,1926:33-34)
26 Hewitt in Hodge (ed.),1907:908
27 Scudiere,1981:63
28 Tooker, Trigger (ed.),1978:424
29 See Smith (1987) for a biography of this man.
30 Jones in Mallery,1893:121
31 Many of these wampum belts are now in museums. The New York State Museum in Albany has 26, including the famous *Hiawatha* belt, dating from circa 1750 and signifying the confederation of the five Iroquois tribes. For a detailed report on these belts, see Clarke,1931:85-121. Recently some 11 belts which had deep cultural, political and spiritual meaning to the Iroquois were transferred from the Museum of the American Indian in New York, back to the Six Nations Reserve in Southern Ontario.(See Nabokov and Easton,1988:48-49)
32 Holm, Suttles (ed.),1990:615
33 The Russian explorer, Bering, visited the northern part of this area as early as 1741.
34 Brotherston,1979:60
35 For a discussion of Levi-Strauss's 'Structuralism' and its application in Northwest Coast art see Sheehan (1978) and Jonaitis (1988).
36 Sheehan,1978:87
37 It should be mentioned that tattoo marks used by the Northwest Coast tribes, are also heraldic designs of the wearer. Thus, with the Haida 'every mark has its meaning; those on the hands and arms of the women indicate the family name, whether they belong to the bear, beaver, wolf, or eagle totems, or any of the family of fishes . . .'. (Swan in Mallery,1893:404)
38 Sheehan,1978:69
39 Levi-Strauss applied the term 'armature' to a combination of properties that remain invariant in two or several myths; extending on this idea, Sheehan (1978:70) suggests that it is possible to use the same term to describe visual elements or properties that remain invariant in a corpus of artifacts.
40 The size of these altars could vary from a few inches to several feet in diameter. The painting always opened to the east.
41 Traditionally, unless certain precautions were observed, the dry-paintings were obliterated. In Pueblo ceremonials, the picture was preserved several days but in the case of the Navajo, it was destroyed within a short time of the completion of the rituals.
42 No permanent copies of the dry-paintings were preserved by the Navajo, the designs being carried in the memories of the Medicine Men who state that the designs have been transmitted unaltered for 'many generations'. (Matthews in Hodge (ed.),1907:404) The Wheelwright Museum in Santa Fe, New Mexico, has an extensive collection of paintings, sketches and drawings of Navajo ceremonial dry-paintings which were collected and documented in the period 1914-58, mainly due to the efforts of Mary C. Wheelwright and Franc Newcomb with the cooperation of *Hasteen Klah*, a Navajo Medicine Man. (See Reichard,1977, for reproductions of many of these dry-painting patterns together with their detailed explanation.)
43 (a) These calendric histories were not exclusive to these tribes. Dempsey (1965:3) refers to one kept by the Blood chief, *Pakap-otokan* or 'Bad Head' and Smith (1960:199-205) records one for the Mandan. However, they are best known for the Sioux (Western, Middle and Eastern) and the Kiowa in part, at least, due to the studies of Mallery (1893) and Mooney (1898).
(b) The Winter Counts of the Sioux were first described by Garrick Mallery in 1876. This was extended to a monumental study in 1893. See Mallery (1886 and 1893).
(c) James Mooney first learned of the Kiowa calendars in 1892 and subsequently published his findings (1898).
44 (a) Dodge,1882:398. Dodge records, somewhat amusingly - but it underlines his persistence in acquiring correct data - his discussions with Stone 'a very intelligent old Cheyenne' relating to counting years among both the Cheyenne and the Sioux: 'We talked of "snows" and "moons", until I fear the old man went off in a state of semi-idiocy . . . at the question, "How many moons are there in a year?" he looked greatly puzzled, evidently never having thought of it before . . .'. (ibid:399)
(b) In Dakota, the word for winter, *waniyetu*, is also the word employed for the English 'year'. (See Howard,1979:6)
45 Smith,1960:201
46 Howard,1960:343 As with today's county clerk, the keepers of Winter Counts sometimes charged a small fee for this service and 'many counts have this fee noted on the count along with the pictographs'. (ibid)
47 Mallery,1893:269
48 It is possible that one of the earliest calendars – before 1832 – was kept by a Kiowa Apache named *Polanyi-katon*, or 'Rabbit Shoulder'. It is speculated that it was buried with him when he died around 1885.
49 As Corbusier noted, the spiral effect is from the center outward 'each year being added to the coil as the snail adds to its whorl - the spiral line frequently seen in etchings on rocks has been explained to me (by Indians) as indicating a snail shell'. (Corbusier,c.1880:1-2)
50 Ewers,1979:xi
51 (a) It will be clear that like all mnemonic devices, the meanings of the symbols were not altogether self-evident and that to be intelligible, each pictograph needs to be accompanied by the data it served to recall. An early leading authority on Sioux Winter Counts, however, observed of the so-called Lone Dog Winter Count that 'every intelligent Dakota of full years to whom the writer has shown it has known what it meant, and many of them knew a large part of the years portrayed' (Mallery,1893:269). As with the pictograph messages referred to earlier, it is clear that the aspect of oral 'literature' coupled with mnemonic devices was highly developed by tribal groups in North America.
(b) Recent researches suggest that Plains Indian ceremonial regalia was sometimes embellished documenting ceremonial. Perhaps among the most complex was the regalia of the owner of a Blackfeet Beaver Bundle, which appears to document the lengthy involved ceremonial, pacing the order of ritual. (See Taylor,1993:71-83)
52 Mooney,1898:144-145

RECREATION AND PASTIMES

1 Strachey, circa 1612, on the football of the Powhatans in McCary, 1957:46
2 Densmore,1979 (reprint):29
3 Underhill,1945:183
4 ibid.
5 Early missionaries reported that they were generally listened to with respect and interest, although questioned and debated with to test their sincerity. It is obvious that Indians saw many parallels between their own genesis myths and those of the white missionaries. See Taylor,1994(a):57-69 for further discussion.
6 Taylor (ed.),1994(b)
7 Smith, Helm (ed.),1981:279
8 Skinner,1911:81
9 Audience participation was desired, thus when Crow myths were related, listeners were expected to answer 'yes' after every sentence or two. When no one replied, it 'was a sign that all had fallen asleep and the story-teller broke off his narrative, possibly to resume it the following night' (Lowie,1918:13).
10 Hilger,1952:115
11 Hilger,1951:108
12 Speck,1935:139
13 Sturtevant and Taylor,1991:192
14 Densmore,1953(a):216
15 Mary-Rousselière, Damas (ed.),1984:440
16 Petersen, Damas (ed.),1984:635
17 Clark,1885:408
18 Ritzenthaler and Ritzenthaler,1970:132
19 Matt and Nellie Two Bulls, the well-known Lakota singers, told me a similar thing. When they composed songs, they retreated to a quiet and secluded place and 'listened to the wind'. They also said – sunderlining the importance of music to the American Indian - 'music is the beautiful thing that we have in our lives' (Discussion, Porcupine, South Dakota, July 1988).
20 Densmore,1953(b):220
21 See Powers (1986) for a detailed discussion of Sacred Language as used in both songs and religious ceremonies.
22 Bowers,1950:111
23 Densmore,1939:256
24 Densmore,1932:162
25 The *pejuta wicasa*, Eagle Shield, said that most of his remedies for adults were received from a bear and one song contained the words 'bear told me about all things' (Densmore,1918:265).
26 Densmore,1918:173
27 ibid:139. Lakota Dream Song sung in Sun Dance by *Zintka la-luta* or 'Red Bird'.
28 McCary,1957:46
29 See, for example, Ewers (1986:159-166) for a discussion of various styles from the Prairie and Plains tribes.
30 Ritzenthaler and Ritzenthaler,1970:131
31 See Taylor (ed.),1995:50
32 Spencer,1959:304 and Blackman, Suttles (ed.),1990:251
33 The water drum was obviously used early. One observer (c. 1700) of the Virginian Indians, recorded 'their musical instruments are chiefly drums and rattles: Their drums are made of a skin stretched over an earthen pot half full of water' (Beverley in McCary,1957:46).
34 See Bates and Gidley in Taylor (ed.),1994(b):73 and 61. In the case of the Mandan, some of the dancers actually wore a single horn fastened to a buffalo robe and slung over the head. See Maximilian, Thwaites (ed.),1906:327.
35 Maximilian, Thwaites (ed.),1906:327
36 Catlin,1841,Vol.I:165. The Buffalo Dance was very widespread and early. It is depicted on a Quapaw buffalo robe (Prairie tribe of the Lower Mississippi) collected prior to 1768 and now in the Musée de l'Homme, Paris (specimen no. R25.34.33.4). A Yankton artist depicted an almost identical scene a century later (N.A.A.76-13,326). In addition to the references in the text, it should be noted that Bodmer also did a single portrait of a Mandan Buffalo Dancer (illus.Taylor,1975:12) as did the Mandan artist *Sih-Chida* 'Yellow Feather', the original of which is in the Joslyn Art Museum, Omaha, Nebraska.
37 Morgan,1901,Vol.I:278
38 To the Iroquois the three primary sources of nourishment were maize, beans and squashes. They regarded these foods as bestowed upon them by the Creator as sacred gifts. They were never abused - especially by waste. (See Speck,1945:38-39.)
39 Tooker, Trigger, (ed.),1978:454
40 ibid.
41 Hewitt in Hodge (ed.),1907:381
42 The Rio Grande Pueblo people ventured to the Great Plains to hunt buffalo. The hunting dances honored the animals and 'also ensured their propagation'. (See Bahti,1970:22.) See also Goldfrank

(ed.),1970:128-139 on hunting ceremonial of the Pueblo of Isleta in New Mexico.

43 The game was borrowed by the whites and played by them under the name of 'bullet' (Culin,1907:339).

44 Mittens were sometimes used instead of moccasins and players among some tribes indicated their choice by pointing with a rod (ibid.).

45 ibid.:267

46 Mooney,1896:1008-1009

47 Culin,1907:389

48 Catlin,1841,Vol.I:141

49 Culin,1907:561

50 Strachey in McCary,1957:46

51 McCary,1957:46-47

52 ibid.:140

53 Catlin,1841,Vol.II:123

54 ibid.:124-125

55 ibid.:125

56 ibid.

57 (a) Minus the elaborate ceremonial accompaniments so characteristic of the Southeast Indians, the Canadians adopted the Ball Game as their national game and called it *La crosse*.
(b) The Choctaw in Oklahoma and Mississippi, proud of their cultural heritage, continue to play the ancient Ball Game as well as performing their ancient dances and songs. See McKee,1989:95.

58 Culin,1907:421

59 Grinnell,1893:183

60 Played in 'chunk yards' by the Cherokee, Creek and other Southeastern tribes. Some were up to 900ft (274m) in length, sunk to 2 or 3ft (61 to 91cm) below the surrounding land and lined with clay to give a smooth flat surface. See Culin,1907:486-488 for further details.

61 Boas,1901:110

62 According to George Dorsey the Plains tribes viewed the netted ring used in the Hoop and Pole game as representing the spider web, mythology relating that it was Spider Woman who controlled the buffalo, producing them from her web. The game, according to the Skidi Pawnee, was originally played as a buffalo-calling ritual. The poles represented young buffalo bulls while the ring was said to be made of the vulva of a buffalo cow. (Dorsey,1904:343)

63 Macfarlan,1958:13

64 See particularly the Origin Myths and All-Powerful Spirits references in Taylor (ed.),1994.

65 The whale actually furnished an important part of the equipment for the game, the ball being made from one of its soft bones. See Macfarlan,1958:258.

66 Fletcher and La Flesche,1911:198

67 Dorsey,1903:12

68 Perhaps the most widely-used embellishment was the hoop (a simple ring, with a cross or netted), which was used as a hair ornament, a cradle charm, or attached to masks, headdresses and 'medicine' cords from tribes as widely spaced as the Crow, Hupa, Cheyenne, Hopi, Oglala and Apache. Meeker suggested that some, if not all, of these objects could be identified with gaming rings (Meeker in Culin,1907:429).

69 Hoffman (1896:127) describes a widespread custom 'The players (in the Menominee racket ball game) frequently hang to the belt the tail of a deer, an antelope, or some other fleet animal, or the wings of swift-flying birds, with the idea that through these they are endowed with the swiftness of the animal'.

THE HOME AND DOMESTIC LIFE

1 Nabokov and Easton,1989:16

2 The first landing of Europeans in Florida was by Juan Ponce de Leon who landed near the site of present-day St. Augustine in 1513, followed by Narvaez in 1528 and then Hernando de Soto in 1539 who was under orders to pacify, conquer and people the land.

3 This term originally referred to any permanent, roofed dwelling made of solid materials. It is possible that the Polar Eskimo actually learned the technique of cutting and building snow blocks from white immigrants in the 19th century, the term *igloo* then being used by non-Eskimos exclusively for the domed snow-block house. See Nabokov and Easton,1989:194

4 There were considerable variations in house styles and even terminology in the Arctic region. See ibid:189-199 for a more detailed discussion.

5 Derived from the Iglukik (Baffin Island), *Qarmaq* or 'hut'.

6 Nabokov and Easton,1989:195

7 Edmund Carpenter on the Iglulik *igloo* ibid:199

8 If a death occurred in the *igloo*, it was believed that the habitation had attracted evil spirits who opposed the living and certain taboos were observed, an extreme one being the abandonment of the *igloo* with the corpse sealed inside.

9 Drying clothes was a vital occupation. Before entering the main living compartment, a *tilugtut* – a small paddle-like implement of wood or bone – was used to beat the clothes free of snow while still in the relatively cold entrance tunnel, otherwise 'if you enter the warm house like that, they will melt and make your clothes wet and heavy'. Freuchen,1961:27

10 ibid:31-32

11 ibid:31

12 Spencer,1959:56

13 Freuchen,1961:30

14 Burch, Jr., Damas (ed.),1984:312

15 ibid

16 Morgan,1965 (Reprint):126

17 Fenton, Trigger (ed.),1978:303

18 Lafitau in Nabokov and Easton,1989:82

19 Morgan,1965 (Reprint):126

20 See Nabokov and Easton (1989:85) for a more detailed discussion of the architectural figures of speech relating to the longhouse in Iroquois oratory, such as 'Secure the doors' which meant that the Mohawks and Senecas should keep a close watch on their territories!

21 Heidenreich, Trigger (ed.),1978:377

22 From the Chippewa *wagin*, 'bent', *o* connective, and *gan*, 'dwelling'.

23 Nabokov and Easton,1989:16

24 Densmore,1979:29

25 It is obvious that the Seminoles and Mikasuki – tribes dislocated and reorganized in the 18th century – owed much to the lifestyles of the original inhabitants such as the Calusa and Timucua, tribes who were all but exterminated by the Spanish. In particular, it is suggested that the idea of thatching with palm leaves, came from the Choctaw and Timucua. See Nabokov and Easton,1989:116

26 A traditional vegetable drink of the Southeastern Indians, it was made with mashed or pounded corn that had been boiled in water. See Garbarino, Porter III (ed.),1989:92

27 The Tigertail family proudly told Nabokov and Easton how their *chickee* stood the ravages of Hurricane Cleo in 1965: 'apartment buildings were leveled while the Indian chickees remained standing' (Nabokov and Easton,1989:120). The author observed the effect of high winds and lashing rain on a small Seminole encampment along the Tamiami Trail in the spring of 1995. Modern walled buildings were damaged and materials scattered. The nearby *chickees*, however, had simply swayed with the wind and rapidly dried out as the storm passed.

28 This type of diet was obviously ancient. For example, analyses of Aleut economic patterns based on faunal debris dating circa AD200, indicated a food pattern of 1.0 part marine invertebrates, 1.8 parts birds, 35.9 parts fish and 51.7 parts sea mammals while terrestrial vegetation apparently 'provided only an insignificant quantity of good in the Aleut diet' (Denniston in McCartney, Damas ed.,1984:131).

29 It was reported that the Creeks partook of the 'Black drink' before councils in order, they believed, to invigorate the mind and body and prepare for thought and debate. Subsequent studies have shown that the plant contains caffeine, the leaves yielding a stimulating beverage with qualities like coffee and tea. See Hough in Hodge (ed.),1907-10.Vol.I:150.

30 (a) I am indebted to our Nez Perce friend, Mylie Lawyer of Lapwai, Idaho, for introducing us to several traditional Plateau Indian foods – including the tasty camas root.
(b) A fascinating essay by Downing and Furniss describes a camas root gathering expedition to the Musselshell Meadow in 1966 and led by Mrs. Elizabeth Wilson, a traditional Nez Perce lady of Kamiah, Idaho (Downing and Furniss,1968).

31 Spinden,1908:204

32 Fowler, D'Azevedo (ed.),1986:65

33 Wedel,1978:1

34 Lewis and Clark, Thwaites (ed.),1904-05.Vol.II:11

35 Charred corn and impressions of corn on burnt clay have been found in the mounds and in the ruins of prehistoric pueblos in the Southwest. See Cyrus Thomas in Hodge (ed.),1907-10.Vol.I:25.

36 Hariot,1893 (Reprint)

37 Speck,1945:85

38 There is some evidence to suggest that some nomadic Plains tribes, such as the Cheyenne and Lakota whose earlier traditional homelands and lifestyle was that of the eastern Woodlands, continued to plant both corn and tobacco on the river bottoms, perhaps even as late as 1850. (i) See Will and Hyde,1964 (Reprint):85. (ii) Discussion with Charles Hanson of Chadron, Nebraska, who showed me areas at the back of his Fur Trade Museum where Brule Lakota probably planted both corn and tobacco (August 1977).

39 It is of interest to note that the preparation of the ground, its location, techniques of planting, care and associated ceremonials, are remarkably similar to those described for Siouan, Iroquoian, Algonquian and Muskogean groups, by chroniclers of the early-17th century period such as Hariot (1893) and Smith (1910) (see McCary,1957). Southwestern pueblos used comparable methods; however since water was limited, they developed extensive irrigation systems, a technology inherited from the earlier Anasazi and Mogollon tribes of the region: see Cordell, Ortiz (ed.),1979:139 who describes irrigation and field systems in Chaco Canyon, New Mexico. For an excellent, concise overview of Pueblo Corn Ceremonials as performed in most of the Rio Grande pueblos, see Bahti, 1970:18-22.

40 Bowers,1965:202-203

41 Wilson,1909:80

42 Wilson,1918:159

43 Will and Hyde,1964 (Reprint):83

44 Gilman and Schneider,1987:33

45 Wilson,1917:23

46 Gilman and Schneider,1987:33-34

47 Wilson,1915:467 and 1917:44

48 Boller, Quaife (ed.),1972:124. Fresh corn was frequently boiled and buffalo or deer marrow spread on it as a 'butter'. The traveler, Boller, describes it as 'very sweet and truly delicious' (ibid:123).

49 Mercy Walker, a Hidatsa woman of New Town, North Dakota, told the author of the use of a mixture of corn, squash, red spotted beans and sunflower seeds which was made into 'corn balls' as a meal for helpers when the *O-kee-pa Pipe Bundle* was opened (Interview, 9 July 1976).

50 Maple sugar was a widely-used commodity in the Northeastern Woodlands. The sap was generally taken from the tree early in the spring, it being tapped by making a horizontal gash in the trunk about 3ft (91cm) above the ground. A wooden spike was then pounded in at an angle so that the sap dripped down into a birch bark bucket. It was then boiled and strained into a wooden granulating trough, being worked with a paddle until it cooled. The granulated sugar was then pulverized and packed into moulds or made into small cakes. Maple sugar was used at feasts in addition to being used on fruits, cereals, vegetables, even fish and meat (Ritzenthaler and Ritzenthaler,1970:13). It was also mixed with warm water to make a refreshing drink. The use of maple sugar was obviously ancient in North America as the Philosophical Transactions of the Royal Society for 1684-85 reported 'the savages have practiced this art longer than any now living among them can remember'.

51 The 'Arts and Crafts' of the various cultural areas has recently been dealt with in this series (Taylor ed.,1995).

TRANSPORT AND TRADE

1 Wood and Liberty (eds.),1980:99

2 Swagerty in Sturtevant (ed.) 1988:351

3 (a) McGuire (in Hodge (ed.), 1907-10.Vol 2:800) makes the point that many of these trails have been obliterated by roads and railways in modern times.
(b) One of the most famous roads between the Plateau to the Plains was the Lolo Trail which runs from Lolo, Montana, to Weippe, Idaho. The Nez Perce name for this route is *Khusahna Ishkit* or 'buffalo trail'. Parts of the trail appear to be thousands of years old: the 'Lolo' is some 140 miles (225km) in length as the crow flies. However, the large numbers of ridges and valleys and natural barriers often 'made the distance three times greater' (Space, 1970:2). I am indebted to Mylie Lawyer (direct descendant of Chief Lawyer of the Nez Perce) for introducing me to the Lolo trail, parts of which I traveled with my family in the summer of 1979, following the route taken by Chief Joseph and his followers more than a century earlier.

4 McGuire, in Hodge (ed.), 1907-10.Vol. 2:800

5 Bishop, 1949:237-238

6 ibid

7 ibid

8 This is considerably faster than band movements using horses on the Plains. Ewers' analysis of data for the Crow Indians from June to September 1805, revealed that daily movements ranged from 3 to 24 miles (5 to 38km) and the median distance traveled 'on the days camp was moved was 91/2 miles' (Denig, Ewers (ed.), 1953:37)

9 On the unavoidable rough terrain of the plains and the Southwest, moccasins had heavy rawhide soles.

10 Denig, 1930:527

11 Hrdlicka in Hodge (ed.), 1907-10.Vol.2:239

12 Denig, 1930:528

13 ibid (a) The Yanktonai Sioux artist, Oscar Howe (1915-1983) obviously inherited these abilities, he almost always being the first to locate arrowheads, beads, game and household objects, mauls, grinders and hide-tanning tools at ancient Indian village sites on the Missouri River - a favorite leisure pastime. (Discussion with Heidi Howe, Vermillion, South Dakota. 15 July 1995)
(b) Captain J. G. Bourke also referred to the impressive ability of Apache scouts 'to hang to the trail by night and by day to pick it out from the rocks and brush, in canon and on precipice'. (Porter, 1986:211)

14 This is the large skin boat or 'woman's boat' of the Eskimo, also spelled *oomiak*. The name derives from Eastern Eskimo dialects. In making long journeys, boat and sled were used alternately - a faster mode of travel than the Woodland portage where intervals between rivers were on foot, carrying a canoe.

15 Spencer, 1959:465

16 ibid:466

17 For a more detailed discussion of this snowshoe complex, see Cinq-Mars and Martin, Sturtevant (ed.), 1981:30

18 The name probably derives from the Micmac, *ababich*, 'thread' or 'cord'; it was traditionally of eel skin. The French Canadians who early made contact with the Eastern Algonquian tribes, abbreviated it to *babiche* with a broader meaning.

19 Spinden, 1974:224

20 Catlin, 1841, Vol.II:139

21 See Taylor, 1994 (c):21

22 Ewers, 1955:306

23 ibid:307 For obvious reasons, *tipis* were limited in size in the pedestrian culture period. At this time, circa 1600, *tipis* were made of six or seven buffalo hides while in the Equestrian Culture Period, on the southern Plains about 1630, some 12 hides were used to make a *tipi* approximately 16ft (5m) in diameter

24 See Taylor, 1994(c):14-27 for a more detailed discussion of these tribal movements.

25 Ewers, 1955:308

26 Grinnell, in Hodge (ed.), 1907-10.Vol.1:569 (a) For more detailed discussion regarding the sacred aspect of the horse to the Plains tribes, see Taylor, 1995 (b).
(b) For a detailed discussion on the impact of the horse on Plains Indian culture, see Ewers, 1955.

27 Grinnell, 1893:236

28 See Sturtevant (ed.), 1989 particularly pp.324-417 which discuss economic relations throughout North America.

29 Tomkins, 1954 (reprint):94

30 ibid

31 Among the most important studies were those by Garrick Mallery in the first *Annual Report of the Bureau of American Ethnology* for 1881. Later, those of W. P. Clark with *The Indian Sign Language* (1885). William Tomkins produced *Universal Indian Sign Language* in 1926, a popular, authoritative volume which also contains a study of the history of the sign language in North America.

32 This is partially based on Mooney in Hodge (ed.), 1907-10.Vol.2:568

33 Fletcher and La Flesche, 1911:432

34 Berlandier, Ewers (ed.), 1969:57 Berlandier also described the Comanche method of smoke-signaling: 'The smoke of a fire, allowed to escape in puffs by removing the burning brands and then suddenly dropping them, its direction, and so on, communicate to other Comanche groups the news of victory or defeat in pursuit of an enemy, the direction an expedition is taking, its progress etc.' (ibid.)

35 Mooney in Hodge (ed.), 1907-10.Vol.2:566

36 ibid See also Fletcher and La Flesche, 1911:434.

37 This idea was obviously suggested by its use by the United States army. General George Crook installed a network of heliograph stations across southern Arizona and New Mexico during the period of the Apache wars (1881-86). The range of each was up to 30 miles (48km). (See Utley, 1973:387)

38 Swagerty, Sturtevant (ed.), 1988:352
39 Lewis, 1986:15
40 Klaus, 1979:131
41 Cartier in Lewis, 1986:9
42 Lafitau, Moore (ed.), 1977:130
43 See Lewis, 1986:33 particularly notes 7-10.
44 ibid:9 Lewis reports that some Indians still preserve maps as part of their cultural tradition and that they sometimes interred them with the dead. One important aspect of indigenous American Indian maps is that they reveal the people's 'spatial structuring and evaluation of the earth's surface'. (Lewis, 1984:92)
45 See Bowers, 1950:32
46 For a more detailed discussion of the use of maps, as well as pictographic messages, by Plains, Plateau and Woodand Indians, see Taylor, 1994(c):169-175.
47 Swagerty, Sturtevant (ed.), 1988:351-352
48 Gibson, Sturtevant (ed.), 1989:376
49 (a) For a discussion of a similar type of trade in the Northeast and, in particular, the impact of Euroamericans on such trade, see Eccles, Sturtevant (ed.), 1988:324-334.
(b) A very good description of trade patterns across the mountains from the Plateau to the Plains is in Teit, Boas (ed.), 1930:358.

THE HUNT AND WAR

1 Wilson,1913:27
2 Wilson, 1913:15-16
3 Wilson,1911:103
4 Gilman and Schneider,1987:72
5 Hilger,1951:120
6 Arima and Dewhirst, Suttles (ed.),1990:395
7 'Nootka Whaling:Man and Nature in British Columbia'. British Columbia Provincial Museum, Victoria, B.C. (no date)
8 Underhill,1945:37
9 See note 7
10 Underhill,1945:41
11 This fish was so oily, that when dried it was used as a candle.
12 It was extracted by pressing the blubber or oily meat under large flat stones.
13 Underhill,1945:16
14 ibid
15 See Sheehan, Taylor (ed.),1994:93
16 Kennedy and Bouchard, Suttles (ed.),1990:331
17 See Taylor,1994(d):67-73 for a discussion of the horned headdress.
18 Ewers,1955:160
19 (a) I have recently described buffalo hunting techniques of the Plains Indians as well as buffalo products, in some detail. See Taylor,1994(c):109-115.
(b) Pemmican was pounded dried meat mixed with melted fat, often with the addition of choke cherries. The word derives from the Cree *pimikan*, 'manufactured grease'.
20 Smith, Helm (ed.),1981:280
21 Smith,1978:68 I am grateful to the late J. G. E. Smith of the Museum of the American Indian, New York, who carried out extended fieldwork among the Chipewyan in the 1960s and 1970s. He related to me several episodes of his experiences among these people and gave me a deep appreciation of their lifestyle. See Smith, Helm (ed.),1981 for more details of Chipewyan culture.
22 The condor, the largest bird in California, was accorded supernatural powers by the tribes that lived there and the feathers were used in sacred ceremonials in much the same way as eagle feathers in other cultural areas. See Bates, Taylor (ed.),1994:78-79.
23 The Zuni had special regard for the feathers **shed** by their captive eagles. Feathers were, however, also plucked from the live bird and formed 'a staple article of trade'. (Fletcher in Hodge ed.,1907-10.Vol.I:410
24 Densmore makes reference to the use of a stuffed skin of a young black bear as the 'eagle catcher's fetish'. (Densmore,1923:60)
25 As Bowers observes (1950:215), according to Mandan belief, the bears had trapped for a long time before the Indians received instruction in trapping. The theory of acquiring this supernatural knowledge conforms to the tribal pattern by which the world of the sacred is brought to the secular world through the medium of a hero.
26 Bowers,1950:214
27 Many of these pole lodges were still to be found in 1932 'even though eagle-trapping was generally discontinued fifty years ago'. (Bowers,1950:233) With the ravages of time, and often fires, many of these lodges have been destroyed. The author, however, has visited at least three in remote areas in old Mandan and Crow territory of North Dakota and Montana at various times in the last 20 years, in company with Stu Conner, Richard Edwards, the late Paul Ewald, Ken Feyhl and Ian West.
28 Densmore,1923:61
29 Ben Benson in Bowers,1950:246
30 Ben Benson in Densmore,1923:62
31 This is known today as Eagle Nose Butte, a high promontory south of Mandan, North Dakota. The author acknowledges the help of the late Paul Ewald of New Town, North Dakota, who in the summer of 1976, took the writer to several Mandan eagle-trapping locations, including the Eagle Nose Butte.
32 Bowers,1950:252-253
33 ibid:253
34 Taylor,1975:15 and 71
35 Catlin (1841.Vol.I:100-101) gives interesting details of the various ways in which scalps were prepared for ceremonial use. He also gives a sketch of 'a man who had been scalped and recovered from the wound'. (ibid:240) A more recent episode was the scalping of William Thompson in 1867, of whom Colonel Irving Dodge said, 'I saw the man some time afterwards, perfectly recovered, but with a horrible looking head' (Thompson attempted to preserve the scalp in a bucket of water until it could be sewn on again). See Taylor, Johnson (ed.),1980:23
36 Marquis,1928:134
37 Some scalps, however, were actually rectangular and were depicted as such in exploit pictographs. See, for example, Grinnell,1896:244.
38 Connell,1985:165
39 Henshaw in Hodge (ed.),1907-10.Vol.II:598
40 Status and position was an important factor in the traditional Northwest Coast social and political organization. Slaves could form up to 30 per cent of the population. See Blackman, Suttles (ed.), 1990:248-250 for an excellent recent discussion of Northwest Coast political and social organization and the position of slaves within the hierarchy of a typical Northwest Coast tribe, the Haida.
41 Laguna, Suttles ed.,1990:216
42 Hough, 1893:625-651 in Hodge (ed.),1907-10.Vol.I:88
43 For a detailed discussion of body armor on the Plains, Plateau and Southwest, see Ewers,1955:204-205.
44 Secoy,1953:74 and Taylor, McCaskill (ed.) ,1989:246
45 One distinguished scholar of American Indian bows concludes that the bow in America was of comparatively recent origin, 'within the last 2,000 years at the very earliest'. He feels this was predated by many thousands of years by the *atlatl*, a throwing stick (Hamilton,1982:13).
46 Thomas Anburey,1791, in Peterson,1971:15
47 Morgan,1901.Vol.II:15
48 Early in the 17th century, the French had established trading posts on the St. Lawrence near Three Rivers. It was to here that the Hurons made annual trading expeditions down the Ottawa River to trade with the French as well as the Montagnais of the lower St. Lawrence.
49 One particularly brutal encounter which completely demoralized the Huron was in March 1649 when the Iroquois destroyed the Huron village of Taenhatentaron and took hundreds of prisoners.
50 Heidenreich, Trigger (ed.),1978:387

RELIGION, CEREMONIAL AND CHANGE

1 La Vonne Brown Ruoff,1990:19
2 Taylor, 1994(a):59
3 This would include such tribes as Chippewa, Menominee and Ottawa in the Woodlands and on the Plains, the Blackfeet, Cheyenne and Arapaho.
4 Detailed studies by the scholar, John Moore, of one Algonquian speaking tribe - the Cheyenne - have identified further layers within these three realms. While no claim was made that these concepts were fully understood by any others than the shamans and priests, when compared with the Christian concepts of heaven and hell, the pattern was far more complex and sophisticated. (See Moore,1974)
5 See DeMalle and Lavenda (1977) for a detailed analysis of Siouan concepts of the sacred. Also Taylor, 1994(a):61-62. Other scholars whom I wish to acknowledge here and who have shared their views on Lakota religion are Mike Cowdrey of San Luis Obispo, California (personal correspondence, March 1995) and Bill Powers of Rutgers University, New Jersey (personal discussions, April 1995).
6 Riggs, 1958
7 See Boas in Hodge (ed.), 1907-10.Vol.II:617
8 Silver, Heizer (ed.), 1978:220-221 Five was the Shasta sacred number.
9 Such as *Wenebojo* of the Chippewa or *Manabush* of the Menomini and Ottawa (Ritzenthaler,1970:138)
10 Petit in Kenton (ed.), 1956:417
11 ibid
12 See Taylor, 1975:12-13
13 Thompson, Tyrrell (ed.), 1916:332
14 Ewers, 1958:139
15 In contrast, Lowie observed, 'You will never hear a Crow boast of his scalps when he recites his deeds'. (Lowie, 1935:218)
16 Wildschut, 1928:419
17 Benedict, 1932:16
18 Mooney, 1891:322 Obviously there is little doubt that in the course of time, even a haphazard use of plants would lead to the natural discovery that certain herbs were effective in the treatment of various symptoms, as Mooney observes, 'These plants would thus come into more frequent use and finally would obtain general recognition in the Indian materia medica'. (ibid:323)
19 Fletcher and La Flesche, 1911:487
20 ibid:488
21 Among the Navajo, such individuals were referred to as *hatali*, 'chanter' or 'singer' and the other *izeelini*, 'maker of medicines', while the Apache called them *taiyin*, 'wonderful', the other *ize*, 'medicine'.
22 Fletcher and La Flesche, 1911:488-489
23 Wissler, 1912:257
24 The idea of extensive materials associated with religious ceremonial was widespread. The Blackfeet Medicine Pipe Bundle, for example, among the most important in their complex bundle system, had much associated equipment - such as a lariat, whip, bowl, saddle and ceremonial costume. (see Taylor, 1993:35)
25 Bahti has made the point that the use of fetishes dates from pre-Columbian times and that the meanings of many of the words used in songs and prayers relating to fetishes are 'unknown today, an indication of an early origin of the use of fetishes'. (Bahti, 1970:5)
26 Wissler, 1912:90
27 Cushing, 1883:9
28 Bahti (1966) in ibid:5
29 This term seems to have been derived from the Chippewa (and other Algonquian dialects) term, *ototeman*, signifying 'his brother-sister kin'.
30 Suttles, Suttles ed., 1990:467
31 It is interesting to note that the Algonquian word, *otenaw* (related to 'totem'), refers to a type of clan patron spirit.
32 Fletcher and La Flesche, 1911:486-487
33 Fenton, Trigger (ed.), 1978:299
34 Also called the New Year's Ceremony and held in January or February, it was the longest of the Iroquois ceremonials, lasting up to one week.
35 See Taylor, 1994(c):67
36 Frigout, Ortiz (ed.), 1979:571
37 (a) *Kachinas* were symbolic representations in human form of the spirits of plants, animals, birds, etc. All Pueblo tribes have *kachinas* but the Hopi and Zuni have the largest number. (see Bahti, 1970:39) Also, for a comprehensive analysis of Hopi *Kachinas*, see Hartmann (1978).
(b) The Spirit Dancers were impersonators of the *Gahan* or 'Mountain Spirits', who were identified with certain mountain tops and caves in the Apache domain. (See Tobert and Pitt, in Taylor ed.,1994(b):32)
38 The term Sun Dance comes from the Sioux as one feature of the occasion was a dance where they looked at the sun. Among such tribes as the Kiowa, Cheyenne and Blackfeet, it was often referred to as the Medicine Lodge ceremony. Associated ceremonials were the *O-kee-pa* (Mandan) and *Massaum* (Cheyenne). (See Mooney (1898), Wissler (1918) and Grinnell (1923)
39 These War God effigies were traditionally carved of wood from trees struck by lightning. Most of these shrines were within a 10-mile (16km) radius of the villages - such as the Twin Mountain in New Mexico. Six hilltop shrines represented the directions and possessed six different kinds of wind. (See Tedlock, 1979:501)
40 Densmore, 1979 (reprint):87 The Chippewa's great concern with curing has found expression in the 20th century with the herbal remedy for cancer called Essiac, which had been obtained from an Ojibwa Indian herbalist in the 1920s. After 10 years of research, Dr. Charles A. Brusch of the Brusch Clinic in Massachusetts and a personal physician of the late John F. Kennedy, reported 'Essiac is a cure for cancer, period'. One of the critical ingredients in Essiac is sheep's sorrel. (Robinson, 1993:3)
41 Densmore, 1979 (reprint):93
42 ibid
43 Speck, 1945:69
44 False Face Society is often used to describe both the False Face Society proper and the Husk Face Society. The former used masks of wood; it was a particularly popular society, more Iroquois belonging to it than to any other society. The masks represented beings seen in dreams or in the forest, while the Husk Face Society tended to evoke the agricultural spirits; both societies put emphasis on curing. (See Tooker, Trigger (ed.), 1978:460)
45 Lyford, 1945:34
46 ibid:35
47 Tooker, Trigger (ed.), 1978:460 See also Fenton, Trigger (ed.), 1978:306
48 See Tooker, Trigger (ed.), 1978:461 (Fig.13)
49 Chamberlain in Hodge (ed.), 1907-10.Vol.I:479
50 For a detailed discussion of the impact of the fur trade in the Colonial Northeast, see Eccles, Washburn (ed.), 1988:324-334.
51 Bell,(1903) in Hodge (ed.), 1907-10.Vol.I:479
52 Eccles, Washburn (ed.), 1988:324 The same author wryly suggests that had this not been insisted upon, the missionaries 'would have been early expelled, if not killed'. (ibid)
53 Agent, 1992:7, and Bailey (ed.), 1995
54 Trigger, Trigger (ed.), 1978:351
55 Taylor, 1994(a):57
56 This impact is discussed in more detail elsewhere. (See Taylor, 1994(a):57 and also Trigger, Trigger (ed.), 1978:351)
57 Obviously Christianity alone did not destroy the Huron confederacy, but there was progressive breakdown of traditional values as Euroamerican technology and Christianity increasingly impacted on the daily life of the tribe (see The Hunt and War:17-18).
58 Iroquois trappers from Quebec introduced various Catholic or Protestant ideas, symbols, and rituals to the Nez Perce and Salish 'prior to the missionaries' arrival'. (Peterson, 1993:83)
59 Peterson, 1993:22
60 In 1667, for example, Jesuit missionaries acted as both witnesses and interpreters to the Treaty of General Peace between the Iroquois (Senecas) and the French. (Trigger, Trigger (ed.), 1978:356)
61 Peterson, 1993:83
62 ibid
63 ibid:Preface
64 ibid:97
65 Taylor, 1994(a):61 I am appreciative of discussions with Jacqueline Peterson-Swagerty (Cody, October 1992) for insights into the impact of missionaries on the culture of the Plains and Plateau tribes. Also additional private correspondence in December 1989.
66 Higbee, 1992:8 This stance of religious accommodation was still practiced on the Northern Plains even as late as the 1940s. Thus, the ethnologist, John Ewers, in reporting on the death of an elderly member of a Blackfeet family, observed that he had 'lighted candles at his head, a Methodist Bible in his hands, and his weather-worn old medicine bundle at his feet'! (Ewers, 1971:141)
67 Peterson, 1993:98
68 ibid:99
69 (a) I have gone back to early sources for this data, e.g. Mooney (1887) in Hodge, 1907-10,Vol.I:248. In recent years there has been much debate as to the number of casualties on the 'Trail of Tears'; possibly, the losses were less than assumed at the time.
(b) In March 1906, the government of the Cherokee Nation came to a final end; the Indian lands were divided and the Cherokee became US citizens.
70 These wars are discussed in more detail in Taylor, 1994(c):209-249.
71 Dempsey, 1972:105
72 Taylor, 1975:118-120
73 Sturtevant and Taylor, 1991:116
74 Press Release. Smithsonian Institution, National Museum of the American Indian, Winter 1989.
75 Office of the Press Secretary, The White House, Washington. November 28, 1989.
76 (a) Discussions with Daniel K. Stevenson (Special Assistant for Institutional Initiatives, Smithsonian Institution, Washington), Hastings. September 1990.
(b) See also *Smithsonian Runner*, a newsletter about Native American activities at the Smithsonian Institution, Washington, 1990 onwards.
(c) These sentiments were expressed to me by Richard West, Jr. at Cooperstown, New York, in July 1995.
76 Taylor, 1975:141

INDEX

PICTURE CREDITS

Author acknowledgements
This book would not have been possible without the immense amount of invaluable anthropological literature and museum resources created and acquired by early field workers among the North American Indians; such sources have been listed in the Bibliography. Extensive travel through American Indian country and research in the ethnological collections has enabled me to gain some first-hand experience of the environment and lifestyle of the indigenous Americans. I am also indebted to many friends both red and white who have shared their knowledge with me.
In particular, in our many years of friendship, John C. Ewers, Ethnologist Emeritus of the Smithsonian Institution, Washington D.C., – who knew the northern Plains tribes in the 1940s when some members remembered the buffalo days and intertribal warfare – has given me invaluable insights into American Indian life. So too have George P. Horsecapture, Mylie Lawyer, Joe Medicine Crow, and Dennis and Rosemary Lessard.
My sincere thanks to my wife Betty, who has yet again helped to create a volume to add to Salamander's library of American Indian titles. And also to editors Christopher Westhorp and Richard Collins, as well as designer Mark Holt, who have done much to bring this book to fruition.

Colin F. Taylor, Hastings, England.

Picture Credits
The publishers would like to thank the numerous museums, art sources, and individuals in the United States, Canada, and the United Kingdom for their help in the preparation of this book and for granting permission to publish their images. The sources are listed below by page, spelt out in full the first time and abbreviated thereafter; artist's names are given where appropriate. Every effort has been made to trace the copyright holders where known. All the photography credited to Salamander Books Ltd was produced by Don Eiler of Richmond, Virginia.

Front Endpaper: Jim Winkley; **Page 1:** Stark Museum of Art (SMA), Orangeville, Texas, ref 42.900/34; **2:** Salamander Books Ltd/Smithsonian Institution (SI), clockwise – 127842 (mat), 038251 (goggles), 313146 (basket), 316910 (spoon), 002701 (comb), 007419 (*ulu*), 418982A (jar), 424871 (doll), 383634 (stick), 011426 (ball), 152844 (moccasins); **5:** Werner Forman Archive (WFA)/Heye Foundation, New York, ref 501/IG0088; **6:** Colorado Historical Society

(CHS), ref F34,488; **7:** (top) Salamander Books Ltd, (bottom) National Anthropological Archive (NAA), Smithsonian Institution, ref 42189-6; **8:** (left) Library of Congress (LoC), ref 61-10229, (right) SMA, ref 82.900/195; **9:** SMA, ref 82.900/441; **10:** (top) Salamander Books Ltd, (bottom) British Columbia Archives & Records Service, neg B-3660; **12:** border – Salamander Books Ltd/Smithsonian Institution (SI), ref 363831; print – NAA, ref 42020-D; **13:** Salamander Books Ltd/SI, ref 75472; **14:** Architect of the Capitol; **15:** NAA, ref N58-10-84-87; **16:** NAA, ref T-13529; **17:** SMA, ref 82.900/306A&B; **18:** (left) NAA, ref 55684, (right) CHS, ref F13977; **19:** Salamander Books Ltd/SI, ref 359032; **20:** NAA, ref 75-5335; **21:** Salamander Books Ltd/SI, ref 175631; **22:** NAA, ref 4708; **23:** (top) Salamander Books Ltd/American Museum of Natural History (AMNH), New York, ref 8725; (bottom) NAA, ref 43126-G; **24:** Collection of Glenbow Museum (GM), Calgary, Alberta, ref P4239-26; **25:** Cheyenne Vision Seekers by Howard Terpning © 1983, Howard Terpning; **26:** border – Salamander Books Ltd/SI, ref 165466; print – Nebraska State Historical Society (NSHS), John Anderson Coll., ref A547; **27:** Salamander Books Ltd/SI, ref A30201; **28:** (top) Salamander Books Ltd/SI, ref 218134, (bottom) Ashmolean Museum (AM), Oxford, ref 1685 B205; **29:** GM, ref unknown; **30:** WFA/Field Museum, ref 502/IG264; **31:** (top) WFA, ref 501/IG0043, (bottom) CHS, ref F36,200; **32:** (top) AM, ref n1836.p21, (bottom) NAA, ref 961-C-1; **33:** WFA, ref 501/IG0133A; **34:** Salamander Books Ltd/SI, ref 020572; **35:** NAA, ref 41106-C; **36:** WFA, ref 502/IG0081; **37:** San Diego Museum of Man (SDMM), ref 1974-2-2; **38:** border – Salamander Books Ltd/SI, ref T01678A; print – NAA, ref 1624; **39:** Salamander Books Ltd/SI, ref 381328; and: Blackfeet Storyteller by Howard Terpning © 1988, Howard Terpning; **41:** NAA, ref 43170; **42:** source unknown; **43:** (top) SDMM, ref 1965-54-2, (bottom) SDMM, ref 1967-104-1; **44:** (left) Salamander Books Ltd/SI, ref 133007, (right) NAA, ref 90-17253; **45:** (top) Salamander Books Ltd/SI, ref 89063, (bottom) Salamander Books Ltd/SI, ref 89070; **46:** (left) Salamander Books Ltd/SI, ref 218053, (right) Übersee Museum, Bremen, ref 14.48; **47:** (top) NAA, ref 2773, (bottom) Salamander Books Ltd/SI, ref 67899; **48:** (top) Museum of New Mexico (MNM), ref 16234, (bottom) Salamander Books Ltd/SI, ref 152913; **49:** (top) Salamander Books Ltd/SI, ref 272975, (bottom left) Salamander Books Ltd/SI, ref 381328, (bottom right) Seth Eastman – Lacrosse Playing Among the Sioux Indians, 1851, oil on canvas, in the Collection of the Corcoran Gallery of Art, Gift of William Wilson

Corcoran; **50:** National Museum of American Art, Washington D.C./Art Resource, New York (NMAA/AR), ref 1985.66.428; **51:** (top) Salamander Books Ltd/SI, ref 128904, (bottom) NAA, ref 2540; **52:** (left) Salamander Books Ltd/SI, ref 234680 (stick) and 234681 (ring), (center) A135260, (right) 216211; **53:** NMAA/AR, ref 1985.66.427; **54:** border – Salamander Books Ltd/SI, ref 362350; print – NAA, ref 90-17238; **55:** SMA, ref 62.900/57; **56:** NAA, ref 55019; **57:** (top), NAA, ref 33370, (bottom) NAA, ref 94-9247; **58:** (top) Canadian Museum of Civilization (CMC), ref 51571, (bottom) WFA, ref 501/ES0169; **59:** (top) American Museum of Natural History, ref 283421, (bottom) WFA, ref 501/ES0281; **60:** NAA, ref 606; **61:** NAA, ref unknown; **62:** NAA, ref 483A; **63:** (top) NAA, ref 55313, (bottom) NAA, ref 45531; **64:** CHS, ref F42582; **65:** Salamander Books Ltd/AMNH (from top to bottom), ref 6037, 5427, 6040, 8741, 8919, 8728; **66:** (top) CHS, ref WHJ 40342, (bottom) Salamander Books Ltd/AMNH, ref 8745, 8844; **67:** Salamander Books Ltd/AMNH, ref 7326; **68:** NAA, ref 76-5690; **69:** (left) CHS, ref WHJ 5709, (right) WFA, ref 501/ES0145A; **70:** border – Salamander Books Ltd/SI, ref 411723; print – NAA, ref 75-4268; **71:** SMA, ref 42.900/42; **72:** (top) CMC, ref 5663, (bottom) SMA, ref 82.900/309A & B; **73:** The Wolf Men by Tom Lovell 1993, © The Greenwich Workshop, Inc.; **74:** NAA, ref 3845; **75:** (top) Salamander Books Ltd/SI, ref 381298 (snowshoes), 381299 (stick), (bottom) NAA, ref 94-9244; **76:** (top) Colin Taylor Collection, (bottom) NAA, ref 347-B; **77:** (top) NAA, 53402-A, (bottom) SMA, ref 62.900/83; **78:** Salamander Books Ltd/SI, ref 154368-1; **79:** (top) NAA, ref T-2810, (bottom) WFA, ref 501/ES0141; **80:** NAA, ref 580-C; **81:** Signals in the Wind by Howard Terpning © 1988, Howard Terpning; **82:** (top) SMA, ref 62.900/41, (bottom) NAA, ref 94-9246; **83:** WFA/Provincial Museum, Victoria, British Columbia, ref 501/IG0307; **84:** SMA, ref 82.900/194; **85:** (left) Salamander Books Ltd/SI, ref 360996, (right) WFA/Alaska Gallery of Eskimo Art, ref 501/ES0138; **86:** border – Salamander Books Ltd/SI, ref 008392; print – NAA, ref 3253-B; **87:** Staatliche Museen zu Berlin, Museum für Völkerkunde; **88:** (top) WFA/Jeffrey F. Myers Coll., ref 501/ES0217, (bottom) Salamander Books Ltd/SI, ref 383131; **89:** (top) NAA, ref 10455-L-1, (bottom) WFA/Provincial Museum, Victoria, British Columbia, ref 501/IG0200; **90:** (top) NAA, ref 36466, (bottom) WFA/Museum of Mankind, London, ref 501/ES0226; **91:** (top) WFA/Field Museum, Chicago, ref 501/IG0393, (bottom) NAA, ref 34,357-D; **92:** (top) Salamander Books Ltd/SI, ref 72643 & 72644, (bottom) NAA, ref 77-8510; **93:** (top) GM, ref P4239-91, (bottom) WFA/Smithsonian Institution, ref

501/ES0151; **94:** Salamander Books Ltd/AMNH, ref 7934 & 7935; **95:** Salamander Books Ltd/SI, ref 357488; **96:** WFA/A. Spohr Coll., Plains Indian Museum, Buffalo Bill Historical Center (BBHC), Cody, Wyoming, ref 502/IG2697; **97:** Salamander Books Ltd/SI, ref 358695; **98:** WFA/Museum of Anthropology, University of British Columbia, ref 501/IG0160; **99:** (top) Salamander Books Ltd/BBHC, (bottom) NAA, ref 215-F; **100:** (left) NAA, ref 3229-B, (right) Salamander Books Ltd/SI, ref 60189; **101:** (left) NAA, ref 1223-A, (right) Salamander Books Ltd/SI, ref 218000; **102:** (top) WFA, ref 501/IG0348, (bottom) NAA, ref 2494-A-2; **103:** (top) Salamander Books Ltd/SI, ref 074437, (bottom) source unknown; **104:** (top) Salamander Books Ltd/SI, ref 08392, (bottom) NAA, ref 3214-C; **105:** (top) NAA, ref 90-17244, (bottom) Kansas State Historical Society, ref Bierstadt no 4; **106:** border – Salamander Books Ltd/SI, ref unknown; print – Arizona Historical Society (AHS), ref 65199 Hanna Coll.; **107:** Salamander Books Ltd/SI, ref 165121; **108:** (top) SDMM, ref 19270, (bottom left) source unknown, (bottom right) North Carolina Historical Society (NCHS), ref N-72-8-399; **109:** WFA/Provincial Museum, Victoria, British Columbia, ref 501/IG0508A; **110:** source unknown; **111:** (left) SDMM, ref Curtis plate 13, (right) Salamander Books Ltd/SI, ref 270816; **112:** (top) NAA, ref 53401-A, (bottom) Milwaukee Public Museum (MPM), ref SWM-1-G-381; **113:** (top) Hamburgisches Museum für Völkerkunde, Hamburg, (bottom) GMC, ref P3064-67; **114:** (top) SMA, ref 82.900/341, (bottom) NCHS, ref N-72-8-392; **115:** NAA, ref 2332B; **116:** Medicine Man of the Cheyenne by Howard Terpning © 1984 The Greenwich Workshop, Inc.; **117:** (top) NAA, ref 476-A-6, (bottom) WFA, ref 502/IG0350; **118:** New York Power Authority; **119:** University of Southern California Library, ref 5614, (bottom) NAA, ref 836; **120:** NAA, ref 3710; **121:** (top) Salamander Books Ltd/SI, ref 165162, (bottom) Salamander Books Ltd/SI, ref 379166; **Back Endpaper:** Jim Winkley.

All artwork produced by Howard Terpning and Tom Lovell has been reproduced with permission from The Greenwich Workshop, Inc. For information on limited edition fine art prints please contact The Greenwich Workshop, Inc., One Greenwich Place, Shelton, CT 06484, USA.

Editors note
The selection and captioning of all illustrations in this book have been the responsibility of Salamander Books Ltd and not of the author.